Independent Schools Examinations Board

MATHS PRACTICE EXERCISES 13+ LEVEL 3 ANSWER BOOK

David E Hanson

Independent Schools Examinations Board

www.galorepark.co.uk

GALORE PARK

Published by ISEB Publications, an imprint of Galore Park Publishing Ltd
19/21 Sayers Lane, Tenterden, Kent TN30 6BW
www.galorepark.co.uk

Design and typesetting Typetechnique
Printed by L.E.G.O. SpA, Italy

ISBN 978 1 907047 77 0

First published 2012

Details of other ISEB Revision Guides for Common Entrance, examination
papers and Galore Park publications are available at www.galorepark.co.uk

Contents

Number

N1 Properties of numbers

1. (a) (1), 2, 3, 6, 7, 14, 21, (42)   (1)

    (b) 3 or 5   (1)

    (c) example 48, 72, 96   (1)

    (d) 53 or 59   (1)

    (e) 16   (1)

    (f) 2   (1)

    (g) 125   (1)

    (h) 2   (1)

2. (i)   36   (1)

    (ii)   4   (1)

    (iii) 39   (1)

    (iv)   47   (1)

    (v)   18   (1)

3. (i)   9   (2)

    (ii) $^-5$ and 5 or $^-2$ and 2   (1)

    (iii) $^-5$ and 8   (2)

    (iv)   (a) $6 + {}^-5 = 1$ (1)

           (b) $5 - {}^-2 = 7$ (1)

           (c) $^-1 \times {}^-4 = 4$ (2)

           (d) $8 \div 2 = 4$ (2)

4. (a) (i)   3   (1)

         (ii)   2   (1)

         (iii) 11   (1)

         (iv)   7   (2)

    (b) (i) $^-12$ (1)

         (ii)   30   (1)

         (iii) $^-8$ (1)

         (iv) $^-3$ (1)

5. (i) (a) 66 (2)

(b) 102 (2)

(ii) 36 (1)

6. (a) (i) 72 (2)

(ii) 10 (1)

(b) $2^2 \times 5 \times 11$ (3)

7. (a) 990 (2)

(b) $2 \times 5 \times 23$ (3)

(c) 484 ($2^2 \times 11^2$) (2)

(d) 5 and 37, 11 and 31, 13 and 29, 19 and 23 (2)

8. (a) 17.8, 17.58, 17.5, 17.35 (2)

(b) 17 (2)

(c) $5^2 \times 17$ (3)

(d) 1188 (2)

(e) 83 and 89 (3)

9. (i) $2^2 \times 3 \times 5 \times 7$ (3)

(ii) 60 ($2^2 \times 3 \times 5$) (2)

10. (a) 25 (1)

(b) $\frac{25}{27}$ (2)

(c) examples 3 and 17, 5 and 19 (1)

(d) $2^4 \times 5^2$ (3)

■■□ 11. 0.22, $\frac{1}{4}$, 26%, $\frac{3}{10}$ (3)

12. (a) (i) 550 (1)

(ii) 1000 (1)

(iii) 48 (1)

(b) (i) 30.7 (1)

(ii) 0.41 (1)

(iii) 210 (1)

(iv) 0.0510 (2)

13. (a) (i)   36   (1)

       (ii) 8   (2)

    (b) (i)   100   (1)

       (ii) 30   (2)

■■□ 14. 0.6 $\frac{5}{9}$, $\frac{27}{50}$, 53% (4)

15. 100   (3)

■■□ 16. (a) 2   (3)

    (b) (i)   3864.5   (1)

       (ii) 131   (2)

    (c) 2.739   (2)

N2 Fractions, decimals, percentages; ratio

1. (a) (i) $\frac{5}{9}$ (1)

       (ii) $\frac{5}{12}$ (2)

    (b) (i) $\frac{32}{40}$ (1)

       (ii) 0.8   (1)

       (iii) 80%   (1)

2. (a) $\frac{4}{9}$ (1)

    (b) (i) $1\frac{3}{4}$ (1)

       (ii) $\frac{15}{4}$ (1)

    (c) (i)   4.6   (2)

       (ii) 85%   (2)

3.   (6)

Fraction (in lowest terms)	Decimal	Percentage
$\frac{2}{5}$	**0.4**	**40%**
$\frac{6}{25}$	**0.24**	24%
$\frac{7}{20}$	0.35	**35%**

4.   (a) examples $\frac{4}{6}$, $\frac{6}{9}$ (2)

    (b) 181.8 cm   (3)

5.   (a) $\frac{12}{25}$ (2)

    (b) $\frac{9}{20}$ (2)

    (c) 62.5%   (2)

6.   (a) $\frac{3}{20}$ (2)

    (b) 0.52   (2)

    (c) £140   (2)

    (d) 5.2 km   (2)

7.   (a) (i) £3.60   (2)

        (ii) £9.10   (2)

    (b) 5%   (2)

8.   (a) (i) 12%   (2)

        (ii) $\frac{22}{25}$ (2)

    (b) (i) Jacket A (A costs £34; B costs £36)   (2)

        (ii) £16   (2)

9.   (a) 39 cases of 'flu   (2)

    (b) (i) 180 kg   (1)

        (ii) 162 kg   (1)

10. (i) (a) £80   (2)

        (b) £480   (1)

    (ii) £456   (3)

11. (i) £116   (2)

    (ii) (a) £174   (1)

        (b) 150%   (2)

12. (i) $\frac{1}{2}$ (3)

    (ii) $\frac{1}{6}$ (2)

13. (a) $\frac{4}{9}$ (1)

    (b) (i) $\frac{2}{3}$ shaded (1)

       (ii) $\frac{1}{3}$ (2)

■■□ 14. (a) $\frac{17}{20}$ (2)

    (b) (i) $\frac{2}{5}$ (2)

       (ii) $\frac{1}{5}$ (2)

■■□ 15. (a) $2\frac{1}{30}$ (2)

    (b) $2\frac{1}{6}$ (2)

    (c) $7\frac{1}{2}$ (2)

■■□ 16. (a) $\frac{11}{15}$ (2)

    (b) $1\frac{1}{6}$ (2)

    (c) $\frac{3}{4}$ (2)

■■■ (d) $2\frac{4}{5}$ (2)

■■■ 17. (a) $3\frac{7}{12}$ (3)

    (b) $2\frac{1}{4}$ (3)

■■■ 18. (a) $2\frac{7}{20}$ (3)

    (b) $1\frac{21}{44}$ (3)

19. (a) £27 (2)

    (b) (i) £22.50 (2)

       (ii) Takings rose by 27 pence.

         He sold 23 (0.92 × 25) burgers at 99p (1.1 × 90p) each, taking £22.77 (4)

20. (i) 7 : 15 (1)

(ii) 7 : 8 (1)

21. (i) 1 : 4 (3 : 12) (1)

(ii) 4 : 5 (1)

(iii) 5 : 3 (1)

■■□ 22. (a) (i) 105 (2)

(ii) 104 (2)

(b) 10 cm (3)

23. (a) £68 (2)

(b) 270 g (2)

■■□ 24. (i) 2 : 5 (2)

(ii) 80 (2)

(iii) $\frac{3}{19}$ (3)

■■□ 25. (i) (a) 14% (1)

(b) 12.5% (2)

(ii) 10 cm (2)

■■■ 26. (i) (a) $1\frac{9}{16}$ (3)

(b) $12\frac{1}{12}$ (3)

(ii) $10\frac{25}{48}$ (3)

■■■ 27. (i) 6 (1)

(ii) $\frac{1}{2}$ (2)

(iii) $8\frac{15}{16}$ (3)

(iv) $1\frac{2}{11}$ (4)

6

Calculations

C1 Mental strategies

1. (a) £59.95 (1)

    (b) 2000 (1)

    (c) 64 (1)

    (d) £32 (1)

    (e) 40 pence (1)

2. (a) £618 (1)

    (b) 1.25 km (1)

    (c) $\frac{7}{10}$ (70%) (1)

    (d) £37 (1)

    (e) order 2 (1)

3. (a) 237 (1)

    (b) £12 (1)

    (c) £63.75 (1)

    (d) 240 (1)

    (e) 08:30 (1)

4. (a) 36 900 (1)

    (b) 16 g (1)

    (c) 300 m (1)

    (d) 32 cm (the same as the original rectangle!) (1)

    (e) 64 tiles (1)

5. (a) 61 (1)

    (b) £210 (1)

    (c) 79 (1)

    (d) 180 g (1)

    (e) 115° (1)

6. (a) $\frac{3}{5}$ (1)

    (b) £7 (1)

    (c) 3550 (1)

    (d) 22 pages (1)

    (e) £6.80 (1)

7. (a) 94 (1)

    (b) 27 sweets (1)

    (c) 40 023 (1)

    (d) 24 pence (1)

    (e) 30 (1)

8. (a) $\frac{4}{7}$ (1)

    (b) £22.10 (1)

    (c) 6 (1)

    (d) £1.50 (1)

    (e) $^-2$ (negative two) (1)

9. (a) 28 (1)

    (b) 1.7 (1)

    (c) 492 (1)

    (d) £230 (1)

    (e) 50 kg (1)

10. (a) £49 (1)

    (b) 3 (1)

    (c) $\frac{1}{5}$ (1)

    (d) 12 (1)

    (e) 300 (1)

11. (a) £2.61 (1)

    (b) 9 (1)

    (c) 64 (1)

    (d) 11 (1)

    (e) 26 (1)

12. (a) 470 cm (1)

(b) ⁻7° Celsius (1)

(c) 24 (1)

(d) (1)

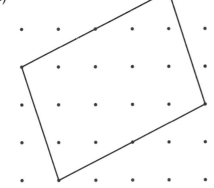

(e) about 75 cm (1)

C2 Written methods

It is expected that working is clearly set out.

1. (a) 16.65 (2)

(b) 5.72 (2)

(c) 285.6 (2)

(d) 10.35 (2)

2. (a) 7.73 (2)

(b) 1.77 (2)

(c) 23.75 (2)

(d) 0.95 (2)

3. (a) 10.07 (2)

(b) 4.89 (2)

(c) 176.4 (2)

(d) 3.6 (2)

4. (a) 7.98 (1)

(b) 2.18 (2)

(c) 14.732 (3)

(d) 1.27 (2)

5. (a) £14.50 (2)

   (b) £2.90 (2)

   (c) £34.80 (2)

   (d) £1.45 (2)

6. (a) 27 (1)

   (b) 53 (3)

7. (a) (i) 166.6 (2)

       (ii) 1.666 (1)

   (b) (i) 3.4 (2)

       (ii) 340 (2)

8. (a) (i) 2383 g (2)

       (ii) 2.383 kg (1)

   (b) (i) 41.5 cm (2)

       (ii) 0.415 m (1)

9. (a) £471.20 (3)

   (b) £7.80 (3)

10. (a) 120.26 (2)

    (b) 98.52 (2)

    (c) 0.6624 (2)

    (d) 11.5 (2)

11. (a) 92.97 (1)

    (b) 60.3 (1)

    (c) 2.352 (2)

    (d) 7 (2)

C3 Calculator methods

1. (i) 10.50 (1)

   (ii) 10 (2)

   (iii) 7.19 (2)

■■□ 2.   (i)   (a) $\dfrac{60}{5 \times 8}$ (2)

             (b)   1.5   (1)

       (ii)   (a)   1.484 001 008   (2)

             (b)   1.48   (1)

             (c)   1.484   (1)

3.   (i)   (a)   £0.41 (41p)   (1)

             (b)   £0.46 (46p)   (2)

       (ii)   £0.43 (43p)   (2)

4.   (i)   1806.79   (2)

       (ii)   1800   (1)

5.   (i)   1.537 313 433   (2)

       (ii)   1.54   (1)

      (iii)   1.537   (1)

6.   (i)   16.689 872 83   (2)

       (ii)   (a)   16.690   (1)

             (b)   20   (1)

7.   (a)   (i)   2931.461 458   (2)

             (ii)   2931.5   (1)

            (iii)   3000   (1)

       (b) $\dfrac{800 \times 0.2}{10 \times 8} = 2$ (3)

8.   (a)   (i)   198.8   (2)

             (ii)   200   (1)

       (b)   20   (2)

       (c)   (i)   2.086 254 782   (2)

             (ii)   2.1   (1)

Solving problems

P1 Reasoning about numbers or shapes

1. (i) $n - 1, n - 2$ (2)

    (ii) $3n - 3 = 54 \rightarrow 3n = 57 \rightarrow n = 19$ (3)

    (iii) 17   (1)

2. 360 (the four scores must be 6, 5, 4 and 3)   (4)

3. (i)   32 cm²   (4)

    (ii) 88 cm²   (2)

4. (i)   (3)

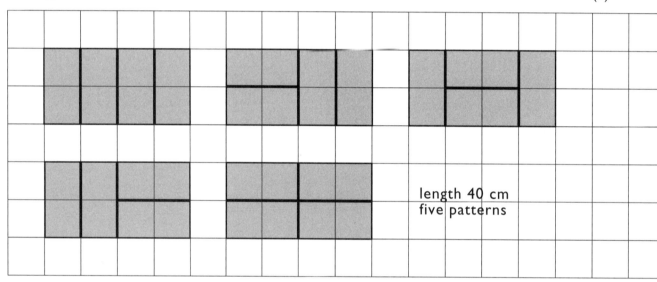

length 40 cm
five patterns

(ii)   (4)

length 50 cm
eight patterns

(iii)   (4)

Length of pattern	Number of possible patterns
10 cm	1
20 cm	2
30 cm	**3**
40 cm	**5**
50 cm	**8**
60 cm	**13**

■■□ 5. (a) (i) 60° (1)

(ii) 120° (1)

(iii) 720° (1)

(b) $16y = 720° \rightarrow y = 45°$ (4)

■■■ 6. (i) (a) 12 (1)

(b) $h - 5$ (2)

(ii) (a) 9 (1)

(b) $h - 8$ (1)

(c) $h - 8 + 9 \rightarrow h + 1$ (2)

(iii) $h = 13$ (2)

7. (i) (a) 54 (1)

(b) 91 (2)

(ii) 33 (3)

8. (i) 24 (2)

(ii) 13.5 (2)

(iii) 4 : 3 (2)

9. (i) (a) 2997 (1)

(b) 0.002 997 002 997 … (2)

(ii) (a) 6993 (1)

(b) 0.006 993 006 993 … (2)

(iii) (a) first and second digits always zero (1)

(b) third digit one less than numerator of fraction (1)

(c) fourth digit always 9 (1)

(d) fifth digit always 9 (1)

(e) sixth digit always 10 minus numerator of fraction
(or sixth digit always 9 minus third digit) (1)

(iv) (a) $n - 1$ (2)

(b) $10 - n$ (2)

10. (i)   (5)

$3^2 - 0^2 =$	$9 - 0 = 9$	(3×3)
$4^2 - 1^2 =$	$16 - 1 = 15$	(3×5)
$5^2 - 2^2 =$	$25 - 4 = \mathbf{21}$	(3×7)
$6^2 - 3^2 =$	$\mathbf{36} - 9 = 27$	(3×9)
$7^2 - 4^2 =$	$\mathbf{49 - 16 = 33}$	$(3 \times \mathbf{11})$
$8^2 - 5^2 =$	$\mathbf{64 - 25 = 39}$	$(3 \times \mathbf{13})$
$9^2 - 6^2 =$	$\mathbf{81 - 36 = 45}$	$(3 \times \mathbf{15})$

   (ii)   all multiples of 3   (2)

   (iii) $3 \times 197 \rightarrow 591$ (for $a^2 - b^2$ in the left column, we have $3(a + b)$ in the
right column)   (3)

11. (i)   125, 230, 423   (3)

   (ii) (a) 13   (1)

       (b) 9   (1)

       (c) 4   (1)

   (iii) Answers vary; example:

      A = 68, B = 125, C = 230, D = 423

      (a) 491   (1)

      (b) 355   (1)

      (c) 136   (1)

   (iv) A = a, B = b, C = c, D = d

      (a) D is $a + b + c$ (1)

      (b) A + D is $2a + b + c$ (1)

      (c) B + C is $b + c$ (1)

      (d) (A + D) − (B + C) is $2a$ (1)

      (e) Answers vary; example: In (ii)(c) and (iii)(c) the answer is twice the value of
A for the group of four terms A, B, C, D. For any group of four consecutive
terms A, B, C, D of the sequence, the value of (A + D) − (B + C) is
always twice the first term (2A).   (2)

15

■■□ 12. (i) (a) x^2 (1)

(b) $\dfrac{x}{4}$ (1)

(ii) $x^2 \div \dfrac{x}{4} = 64 \rightarrow \dfrac{4x^2}{x} = 64 \rightarrow 4x = 64 \rightarrow x = 16$ (3)

13. (i) 899 (1)

(ii) 23 and 37 (23 × 37 = 851) (3)

14. (i) (a) even (1)

(b) even (1)

(c) even (1)

(ii) (a) odd (1)

(b) even (1)

(iii) even (1)

(iv) $x = 8, y = 6, z = 3$ (3)

15. (i) shapes with area 16 cm²

     (a) parallelogram (1)

     (b) kite (2)

     (c) isosceles triangle (2)

  (ii) shapes with perimeter 16 cm

     (a) rectangle (1)

     (b) parallelogram (3)

     (c) isosceles triangle (3)

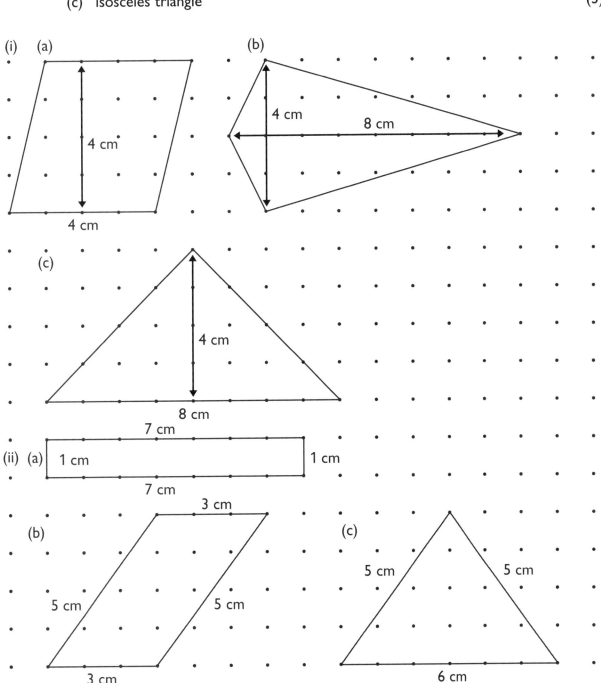

16. (i) (2)

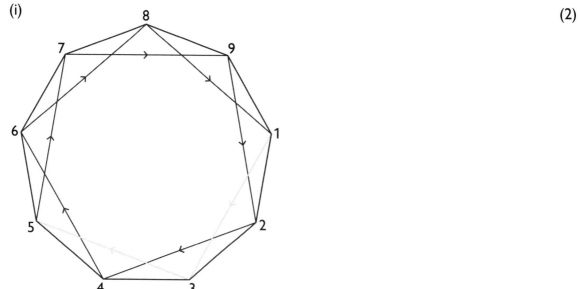

(ii) (2)

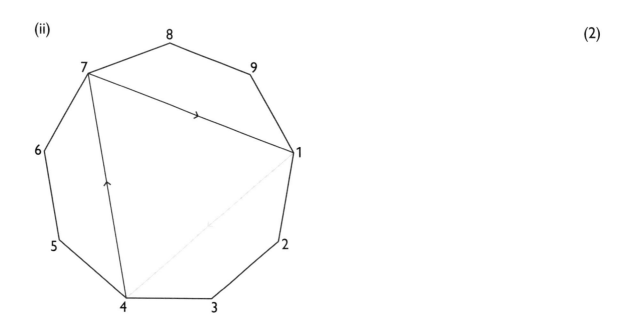

(iii) (2)

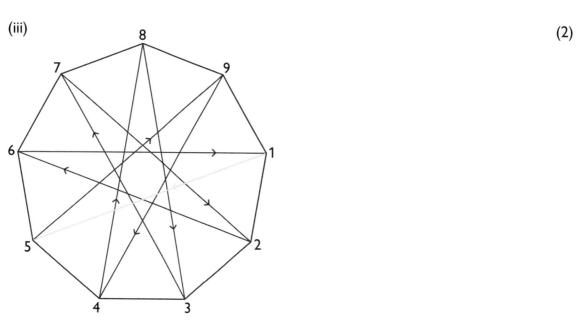

(iv) (a)   (2)

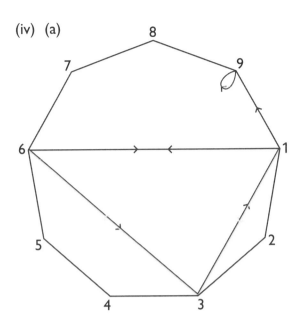

(b)   1   3   6   1   6   **3**   **1**   **9**   **9**   (4)

Boy 9 eventually throws it to himself!

17. (i) (a) 48 → 24 → 12 → 6   (1)

     (b) 45 → 46 → 23 → 24 → 12 → 6   (1)

     (ii) (a) double each time   (1)

     (b) multiply by 2 and then subtract 1   (2)

     (iii) a = 145, b = 160, c = 16   (3)

     (iv) Answers vary; example:

     150 → 75 → 76 → 38 → 19 → 20 → 10 → 5   (3)

18. (i) (a) 53 → 23 → 11 → 3   (1)

     (b) 81 → 17 → 15 → 11 → 3   (1)

     (c) 76 → 55 → 35 → 23 → 11 → 3   (1)

     (d) 18 → 17 → 15 → 11 → 3   (1)

     (ii) Answers vary; examples:

     18 and 81 follow the same route.

     The order of the digits makes no difference to the result.   (1)

     (iii) (a) 29 → 29   (1)

     (b) 59 → 59   (1)

     (c) 95 → 59   (1)

(iv) These numbers have only one stage and do not reach a single-digit number. (1)

(v) 34, 39, 43 and 45 (4)

(vi) 79 (2)

■■■ 19. Tom's number is 13 (6)

■■■ 20. (i) gaps filled in with missing palindromic prime numbers

11 **101** 131 **151** 181 **191** 313 **353** 373 **383** (5)

(ii) (a) all other two-digit palindromic numbers are multiples of 11 (1)

(b) they would all be even (end in 2) (1)

(c) they would be even or multiples of 5 (2)

(d) 707 divides by 7 (1)

(e) 717 divides by 3 (1)

P2 Real-life mathematics

1. (a) £21.89 (2)

(b) (i) £29.46 (2)

(ii) £20.54 (2)

(c) £11.50 (2)

2. (i) (a) 56 m (1)

(b) 192 m^2 (1)

(ii) (a) 10.5 m (1)

(b) 183.75 m^2 (3)

3. (a) $\frac{1}{3}$ (2)

(b) $\frac{5}{12}$ (2)

(c) (i) 7 (1)

(ii) 6 (1)

4. (i) List completed: 225 pence, 49 pence, 3 kg (3)

(ii) 12 kg (1)

(iii) £6.40 (2)

(iv) 53 pence per kilogram (2)

5. (i) 3240 g (2)

(ii) (a) 1600 ml (2)

(b) 8 eggs (2)

(c) 1280 g (1.28 kg) (2)

(d) 1.6 kg (1600 g) (2)

6. (i) £392 (2)

(ii) (a) £95 (1)

(b) 19% (2)

7. (i) (a) $x + 7$ (1)

(b) $2x + 5$ (1)

(ii) $2x + 5 = x + 10$ (2)

(iii) $x = 5$ (2)

(iv) 12 tokens (Anne has 12; Belinda has 15) (2)

■■□ 8. (a) (i) 50 m/s (3)

(ii) 110 miles/hour (2)

(b) 12:40 (4)

9. (a) 45 cm (2)

(b) £15 (4)

10. (i) 50 copies (2)

(ii) (a) 3.2 cm (2)

(b) 37 copies ($37\frac{1}{2}$ so there is not room for 38 copies!) (3)

11. (i) (a) range 7 centimetres (1)

(b) range 13 square centimetres (1)

(c) median 40 cm (1)

(d) median 112 cm^2 (1)

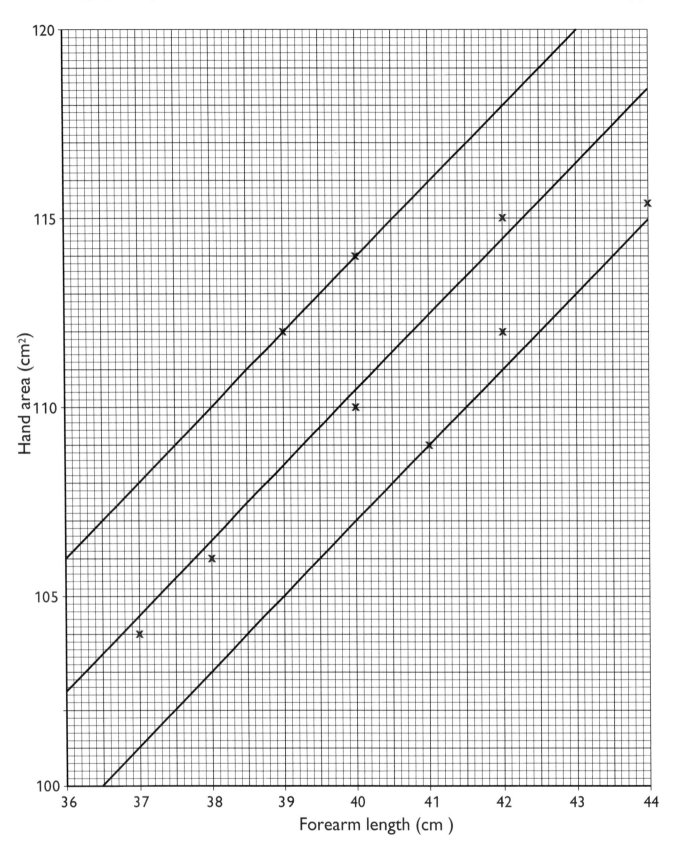

(iii) positive (and fairly high) correlation   (2)

■■□ (iv) (a) line of best fit drawn (1)

(b) parallel lines drawn (2)

(v) (a) about 99 cm^2 (1)

(b) about 106 cm^2 (1)

(vi) Shanna's hand area approximately 100 cm^2 (3)

12. (i) 250 miles (2)

(ii) 84 litres (2)

(iii) 240 miles (2)

(iv) 28 litres (2)

13. (i) $\frac{5}{6}$ (2)

(ii) $\frac{1}{6}$ (1)

(iii) 54 (number must be a multiple of 6) (2)

(iv) Charles took 9 more stamps than Hannah. (2)

14. (i) (a) $\frac{1}{10}$ (1)

(b) $\frac{3}{10}$ (1)

(ii) $\frac{3}{5}$ (1)

(iii) $\frac{9}{20}$ (2)

(iv) 80 (2)

(v) (3)

Grade	A	B	C	D	E
Number of candidates	8	24	36	5	7

15. (i) 252 (2)

(ii) 450 (1)

(iii) 5 : 4 (2)

(iv) $\frac{4}{9}$ (2)

(v) 56% (2)

16. (i) 8 km (1)

(ii) 15 litres (1)

(iii) 144 km (1)

(iv) 54 litres (2)

(v) £67.50 (3)

■■□ 17. (i) 90 cm (88 cm + 2 cm) (3)

(ii) 616 cm^2 (3)

(iii) 4312 cm^3 (2)

(iv) 5488 cm^3 (2)

■■□ 18. (a) (i) 140 metres (1)

(ii) 714 complete revolutions (1)

(b) (i) 22.5 km (22 500 metres) (2)

(ii) 9.5 tonnes (9500 kg) (2)

19. (i) 16 m^2 (1)

(ii) 4.8 m^3 (2)

(iii) 9 m^2 (3)

■■□ 20. (i) 154 cm^2 (3)

(ii) (a) 784 cm^2 (1)

(b) 308 cm^2 (2)

(c) 476 cm^2 (2)

(iii) 39% (2)

21. (i) 5 cm (1)

(ii) (a) $20x - 200$ or $20(x - 10)$ cm^2 (2)

(b) $(30x - 100)$ cm^2 (4)

(iii) (a) $x = 48$ (2)

(b) 1340 cm^2 (0.134 m^2) (2)

24

22. (i) (a) 500 m   (2)

      (b) $\frac{1}{2}$ km (0.5 km)   (1)

   (ii) $2\frac{1}{4}$ km (2.25 km)   (2)

   (iii) 27 minutes   (3)

■■□ 23. (i) 1500 litres (1.5 m^3)   (3)

   (ii) 75 days   (3)

   (iii) (a) 100 litres   (1)

      (b) 1.4 m   (3)

24. (i) 81 000   (2)

   (ii) 24 300   (2)

   (iii) 32 400 (England had 56 700 supporters)   (2)

25. (i) 1.6 g   (2)

   (ii) (a) 400 cm^2 (1)

      (b) 360 cm^2 (1)

   (iii) (a) 6.4 g   (2)

      (b) 5.76 g   (2)

26. (i) 22 litres   (2)

   (ii) 585 miles   (2)

   (iii) 26 litres   (2)

27. (i) 9 screws   (1)

   (ii) 17 screws   (2)

   (iii) 38 screws   (3)

   (iv) 57 screws   (2)

   (v) 121 screws   (1)

Algebra

A1 Equations and formulae

1. (a) $3a$ (1)

   (b) a (1)

   (c) $4a$ (1)

   (d) $2a^2$ (1)

   (e) a (1)

2. (a) $2a$ (1)

   (b) 0 (2)

   (c) $10c^3$ (2)

   (d) $2d$ (2)

3. (a) $6d$ (1)

   (b) $5d$ (1)

   (c) $12d^2$ (2)

   (d) $4d$ (1)

4. (a) $4m - 4$ (2)

   (b) $4(m - 1)$ (2)

5. (a) (i) $11y$ (1)

       (ii) $21y^3$ (2)

       (iii) $2y^2$ (1)

   (b) $6p - q$ (3)

   (c) $6(2a + 3b)$ (2)

6. (a) (i) $7p$ (1)

       (ii) $12p^2$ (2)

       (iii) p (2)

   (b) $3(3p - 2)$ (2)

7.   (a) $13a$ (1)

       (b) ^-3a (2)

       (c) $40a^2$ (2)

       (d) $4a$ (2)

       (e) $25a^2$ (2)

8.   (a) $2a + 23c$ (3)

       (b) $5p(p - 2q)$ (2)

9.   (a) $3a + 7b$ (1)

       (b) $6a^2b$ (1)

       (c) ^-c (2)

       (d) $2d$ (2)

       (e) $6e^5$ (2)

■■□   (f) $6e^2$ (2)

10.   (a) $5x^2 - x^3$ (2)

       (b) $30x^2$ (2)

■■□   (c) 2 (2)

11.   (a)   (i) $5x^3$ (1)

            (ii) $6x^6$ (2)

■■■   (iii) $\dfrac{2x^2}{y^3}$ (2)

       (b)   (i) $2s(s + 1)$ (2)

            (ii) $2r(2r - 3s)$ (2)

12.   (a) $3x - y$ (3)

       (b)   (i) $6a^2$ (2)

■■■   (ii) b (2)

■■■   (c) $5a^2(a - 1)$ (2)

13.   (a) $6a + 13$ (3)

       (b)   (i) $2(2a + 7)$ (1)

■■■   (ii) $\pi r(6 + r)$ (3)

14.   (a) $5p + 2q$ (2)

        (b)   (i) $4p^2q^3$ (2)

             (ii) $\dfrac{3p^2}{2q}$ (3)

15.   (a) $\dfrac{3x - 12}{4x}$ (2)

        (b) $2xy$ (2)

16.   (i)   13   (2)

        (ii)   10   (2)

        (iii) $^-7$ (2)

17.   (i)   13   (2)

        (ii)   4   (2)

        (iii) $^-6$ (2)

18.   (i)   16   (2)

        (ii)   15   (2)

        (iii) $^-96$ (3)

19.   (i) $^-1$ (2)

        (ii) $^-10$ (2)

        (iii) $^-12$ (2)

20.   (i)   3   (2)

        (ii)   0   (2)

        (iii) $^-3$ (2)

        (iv) $^-12$ (3)

21.   (i)   0   (1)

        (ii)   8   (2)

        (iii) $^-18$ (2)

■■□ 22.   (a)   (i)   0.64   (2)

             (ii)   1.06   (3)

        (b)   4.2 unit^2 (3)

■■□ 23. (a) (i) $^-0.2$ (2)

(ii) $^-2.24$ (2)

(b) 46.2 cm³ (3)

24. (i) (a) $4t$ (1)

(b) $4t + 4$ (1)

(ii) $4t + 4 = 44$ (2)

(iii) $t = 10$ (2)

(iv) 30 years (2)

25. (i) $n - 4$ (1)

(ii) (a) $5n$ (1)

(b) $7n - 4$ (2)

(iii) $n = 2$ (2)

26. (i) $\dfrac{x}{2}$ (1)

(ii) $\dfrac{x}{2} + 30$ (1)

(iii) $x + \dfrac{x}{2} + (\dfrac{x}{2} + 30)$ which simplifies to $2x + 30$ (2)

(iv) $2x + 30 = 180 \rightarrow x = 75$ (2)

(v) (a) angle Q is 37.5° (1)

(b) angle R is 67.5° (1)

27. (i) cn (pence) (1)

(ii) (a) $c - 5 = d$ (2)

(b) $c = 14$ (2)

(iii) $n = 39$ (pence) (2)

(iv) £5.46 (1)

28. (i) (a) $r + 3$ (1)

(b) $4r$ (1)

(ii) (a) $6r + 3$ (2)

(b) $2r + 1$ (2)

29

(iii) $2r + 1 = 11 \rightarrow r = 5$ (3)

(iv) 5, 8, 20   (1)

29. (i) 2 : 3   (2)

(ii) (a) $2x$ (1)

(b) $3x$ (1)

(iii) $\frac{2}{3}$ (2)

(iv) (a) 42   (2)

(b) 14   (2)

30. (a) $w = 9$ (1)

(b) $x = 4$ (1)

(c) $y = 8$ (2)

(d) $z = 3$ (2)

31. (a) $a = 5$ (1)

(b) $b = 48$ (2)

(c) $c = 3$ (2)

(d) $d = 6$ (3)

32. (a) $w = 15$ (1)

(b) $x = 7$ (2)

(c) $y = 8$ (2)

(d) $z = {}^-2$ (3)

■■□ 33. (a) $v = 3$ (1)

(b) $w = 49$ (2)

(c) $x = 10$ (2)

(d) $y = {}^-18$ (3)

■■□ 34. (a) $x = {}^-6$ (2)

(b) $y = 3$ (2)

(c) $z = 5$ (3)

■■□ 35. (a) $x = 10$ (1)

(b) $y = 4$ (2)

(c) $z = 7$ (2)

■■□ 36. $z = 14$ (4)

■■□ 37. (a) $p = {}^-1$ (1)

(b) $q = 3\frac{1}{2}$ (2)

(c) $r = 20$ (2)

(d) $s = 3$ (3)

■■□ 38. (a) $x = 11$ (2)

(b) $y = 10$ (2)

(c) $z = {}^-\frac{1}{4}$ (2)

■■■ 39. (a) $a = 5$ (2)

(b) $b = 10\frac{1}{2}$ (2)

(c) $c = 11$ (3)

■■■ 40. (a) (i) $x = 18$ (2)

(ii) $y = {}^-3$ (3)

(iii) $z = 17$ (3)

(b) (i) $a > 2$ (2)

(ii) $b < 10\frac{2}{3}$ (3)

■■■ 41. (a) (i) $x \leq 8$ (2)

(ii) $1, 2, 3, 4, 5, 6, 7, 8$ (2)

(b) (i) $x > 4$ (2)

(ii) $5, 6, 7, 8$ (2)

■■■ 42. (i) $x > {}^-3$ (2)

(ii) ${}^-2, {}^-1$ (2)

■■■ 43. (a) $x = 2$ (2)

(b) (i) $p < 6\frac{2}{3}$ (2)

(ii) $1, 2, 3, 4, 5, 6$ (1)

■■■ 44. (i) (a) $x < 3$ (2)

(b) $x \geq {}^-2$ (3)

(ii) ${}^-2, {}^-1, 0, 1, 2$ (1)

■■■ 45. (a) (i) $2a^2$ (2)

(ii) 1 (2)

(b) $4a(2a + 3)$ (2)

(c) $9a - 26b$ (2)

(d) (i) $a < 3\frac{1}{5}$ (2)

(ii) 1, 2, 3 (1)

■■■ 46. (a) (i) $x = 28$ (2)

(ii) $w = 5\frac{1}{3}$ (2)

(b) $4x^2 - 5x + 18$ (4)

(c) (i) $x > 4\frac{1}{2}$ (3)

(ii) $x \leq 12$ (3)

(iii) number line drawn (2)

■■■ 47. $x = 5.91$ (4)

■■■ 48. $x = 1.53$ (5)

■■■ 49. $x = 7$ or $x = 3$ (5)

■■■ 50. (i) (a) $w + 5.3$ (1)

(b) $w(w + 5.3)$ (2)

(ii) (a) 9.78 cm (4)

(b) 28.52 cm (3)

■■■ 51. (i) (a) $\dfrac{48}{b}$ (2)

(b) $\dfrac{48}{b} - b$ (3)

(ii) (a) 2.4 (2)

(b) 20 (1)

(c) 17.6 (1)

■■■ 52. (i) $x + 4$ (1)

(ii) $x(x + 4) \rightarrow x^2 + 4x$ (2)

(iii) $x^2 + 4x = 50 \rightarrow x = 5.35$ (5)

■■■ 53. (a) $x = 2.5$ cm (3)

(b) (i) 2 faces area $x(x - 2) \rightarrow 2x^2 - 4x$

2 faces area $4(x - 2) \rightarrow 8x - 16$

2 faces area $4x \rightarrow 8x$

total surface area $2x^2 + 12x - 16$ (4)

(ii) $2x^2 + 12x - 16 = 94 \rightarrow 2x^2 + 12x - 110 = 0$ (1)

(iii) $x = 5$ (the second solution to this equation, $^-11$, is not appropriate in this case! (3)

■■■ 54. (i) (a) $x < 8\frac{1}{3}$ (2)

(b) $x \geq {}^-6$ (2)

(ii) $^-6, {}^-5, {}^-4, {}^-3, {}^-2, {}^-1, 0, 1, 2, 3, 4, 5, 6, 7, 8$ (3)

■■■ 55. (i) $x(5x + 2)$ (2)

(ii) $x = {}^-2$ and $x = 1.6$ (8)

56. (a) $2x(2x + 1)$ (2)

(b) $^-2.78$ (6)

A2 Sequences and functions

1.   (a)   29, 23   (2)

    (b)   21, 25   (2)

    (c)   16, 8   (2)

2.   (a) (i)   24   (1)

         (ii)   32   (1)

    (b) (i)   19   (1)

         (ii)   25   (1)

    (c) (i)   21   (2)

         (ii)   144   (2)

3.   (a)   30, 37   (2)

    (b)   81, 243   (2)

    (c) $3\frac{1}{2}$, $1\frac{1}{4}$ (4)

4.   (a)   126, 626, 3126   (3)

    (b)   (4), 6, 12, 30, 84   (4)

5.   (a) $\frac{6}{7}$, $\frac{5}{6}$ (2)

    (b)   35, 17   (2)

    (c)   111, 37   (2)

6.   (a) (i)   27, 35   (2)

         (ii)   100, 144   (2)

         (iii)   23, 37   (2)

    (b) (i)   16   (1)

         (ii)   28   (1)

         (iii) $3n - 2$ (2)

         (iv)   298   (2)

7. (i) 17, 20 (1)

(ii) $3n + 2$ (2)

(iii) 62 (1)

(iv) 41 (2)

(v) 333rd term = 1001 (2)

8. (i) (a) $^-4$ (1)

(b) 9995 (1)

(ii) $n = 23$ (2)

9. (i) (a) $\frac{1}{7}$ (1)

(b) $\frac{199}{601}$ (1)

(ii) t_n approaches $\frac{1}{3}$ (2)

10. (i) $\dfrac{10^2}{4} \rightarrow \dfrac{100}{4} \rightarrow 25$ (2)

(ii)

T_n	sequence	1st difference sequence	nth term of 1st difference	2nd difference constant	
$\frac{1}{4}n$	$\frac{1}{4}, 1, 2\frac{1}{4}, 4, \ldots$	$\frac{3}{4}, 1\frac{1}{4}, 1\frac{3}{4}, \ldots$	$\frac{1}{2}\left(n + \frac{1}{2}\right)$	$\frac{1}{2}$	
$\frac{1}{2}n$	$\frac{1}{2}, 2, 4\frac{1}{2}, 8, \ldots$	$1\frac{1}{2}, 2\frac{1}{2}, 3\frac{1}{2}, \ldots$	$n + \frac{1}{2}$	1	
n^2	1, 4, 9, 16, ...	3, 5, 7, ...	$2n + 1$	2	(4)
$2n^2$	2, 8, 18, 32, ...	6, 10, 16, ...	$4n + 2$	4	(4)

11. (a) $x = 3$ drawn and labelled on grid (1)

(b) $y = 5$ drawn and labelled (1)

(c) $x = {}^-4$ drawn and labelled (1)

(d) $y = x$ drawn and labelled (2)

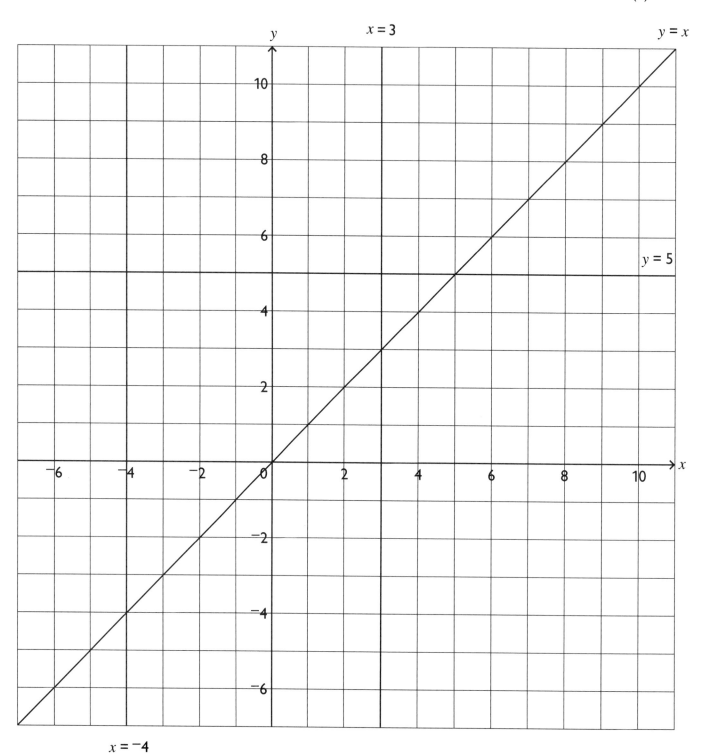

12. (i) (a)

x	-3	0	3
y	**0**	**3**	**6**

(2)

   (b) graph of $y = x + 3$ drawn on grid

(2)

(ii) (a)

x	-3	0	3
y	**8**	**5**	**2**

(2)

   (b) graph of $y = 5 - x$ drawn on grid

(1)

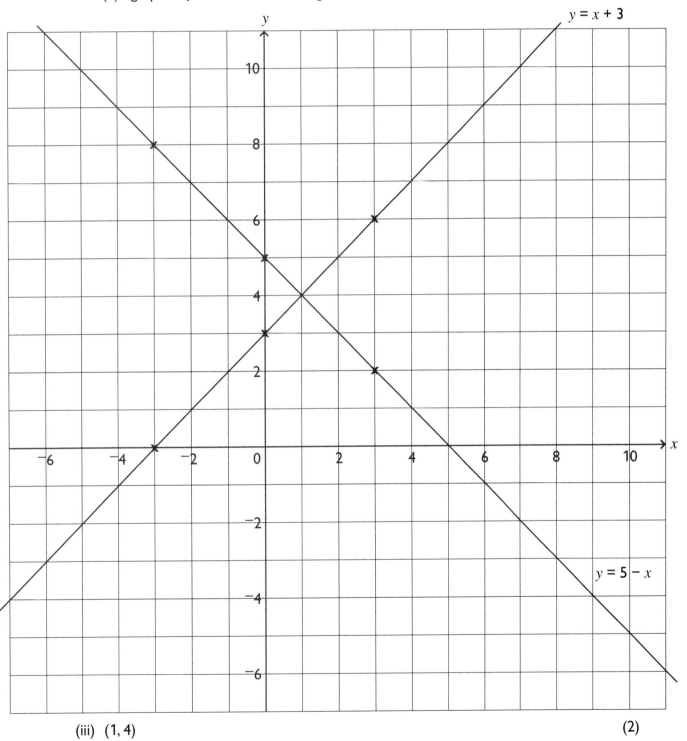

(iii) (1, 4)

(2)

13. (i) (a)

x	$^-2$	1	4
y	$^-1$	2	5

(2)

(b)

x	$^-2$	1	4
y	9	6	3

(2)

(ii) (a) graph of $y = x + 1$ drawn (1)

(b) graph of $y = 7 - x$ drawn (2)

(iii) line $y = 1$ drawn (1)

(iv) 4 points circled (2)

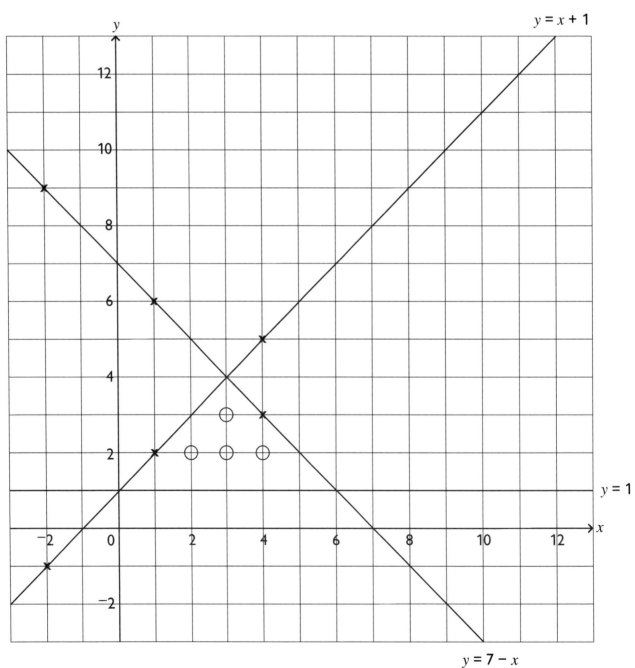

38

14. (i) answers vary; examples $(0, 3)$, $(2, 1)$ (2)

(ii) $y = {}^-1$ (1)

(iii) (a) (2)

x	$^-1$	0	1	2	x
y	1	3	5	7	$2x + 3$

(b) $y = 2x + 3$ (1)

(c) line C ($y = 2x + 3$) drawn (2)

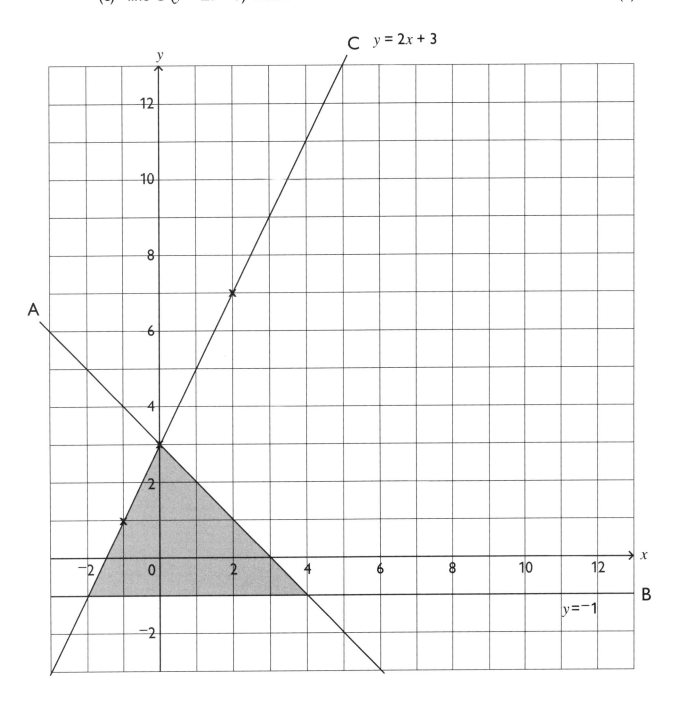

(iv) 12 cm² (3)

■■■ 15. (i)

x	−3	−2	−1	0	1	2	3	(2)
y	9	4	1	0	1	4	9	

(ii) graph of $y = x^2$ drawn (2)

(iii) $y = 7$ drawn (1)

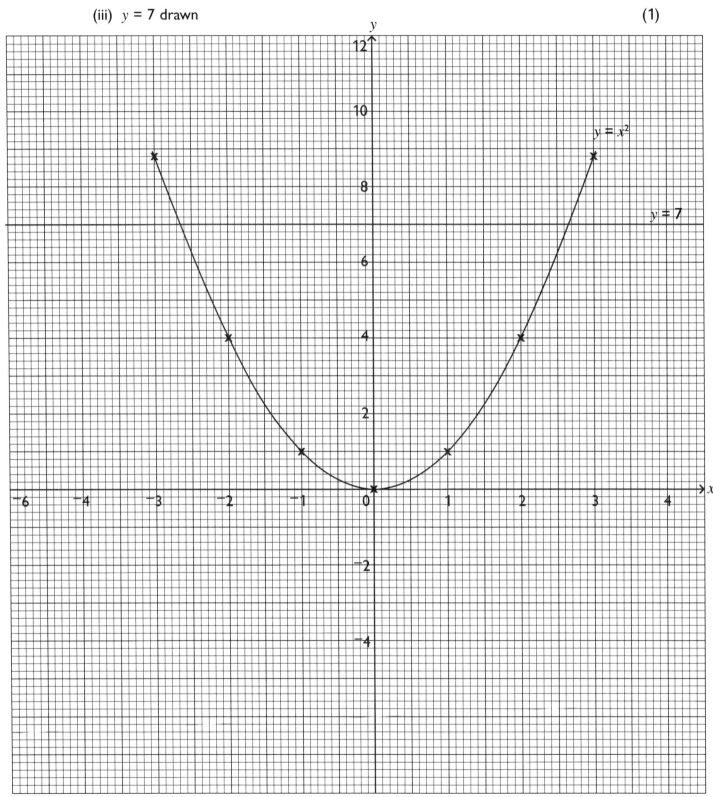

(iv) 2.65 (1)

■■■ 16. (i) (2)

x	$^-3$	$^-2$	$^-1$	0	1	2	3
y	7	2	$^-1$	$^-2$	$^-1$	2	7

(ii) graph of $y = x^2 - 2$ drawn (2)

(iii) $y = x$ drawn (2)

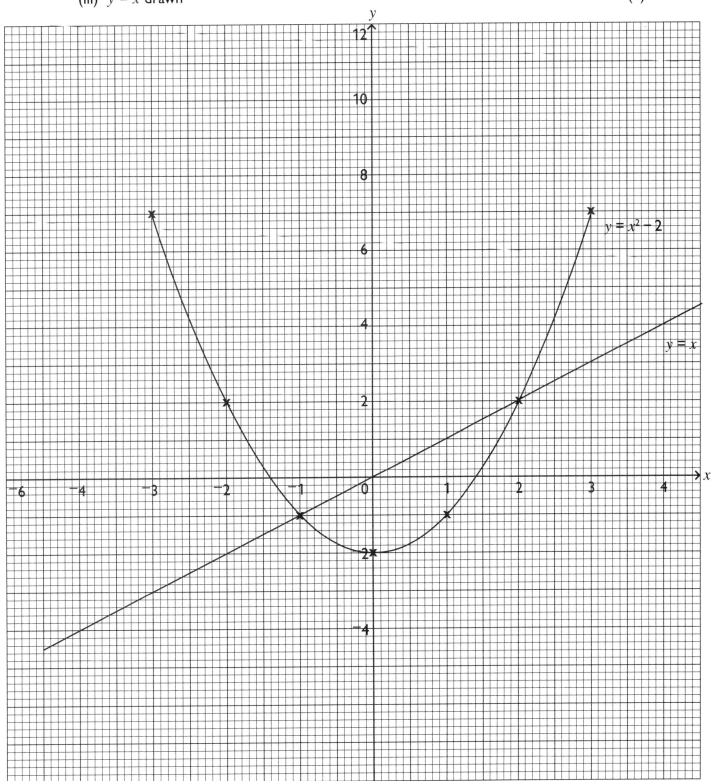

(iv) $(^-1, ^-1), (2, 2)$ (2)

■■■ 17. (i)

x	$^-3$	$^-2$	$^-1$	0	1	2	3	4	(3)
$\frac{1}{2}x^2$	**4.5**	**2**	**0.5**	**0**	0.5	**2**	4.5	**8**	
y	**1.5**	$^-$**1**	$^-$**2.5**	$^-$**3**	$^-$**2.5**	$^-$**1**	**1.5**	**5**	

(ii) graph of $y = \frac{1}{2}x^2 - 3$ drawn (2)

(iii) graph of $y = x - 1$ drawn (3)

(iv) points circled (see graph over page) (1)

(v) $(1, ^-2)$ (1)

42

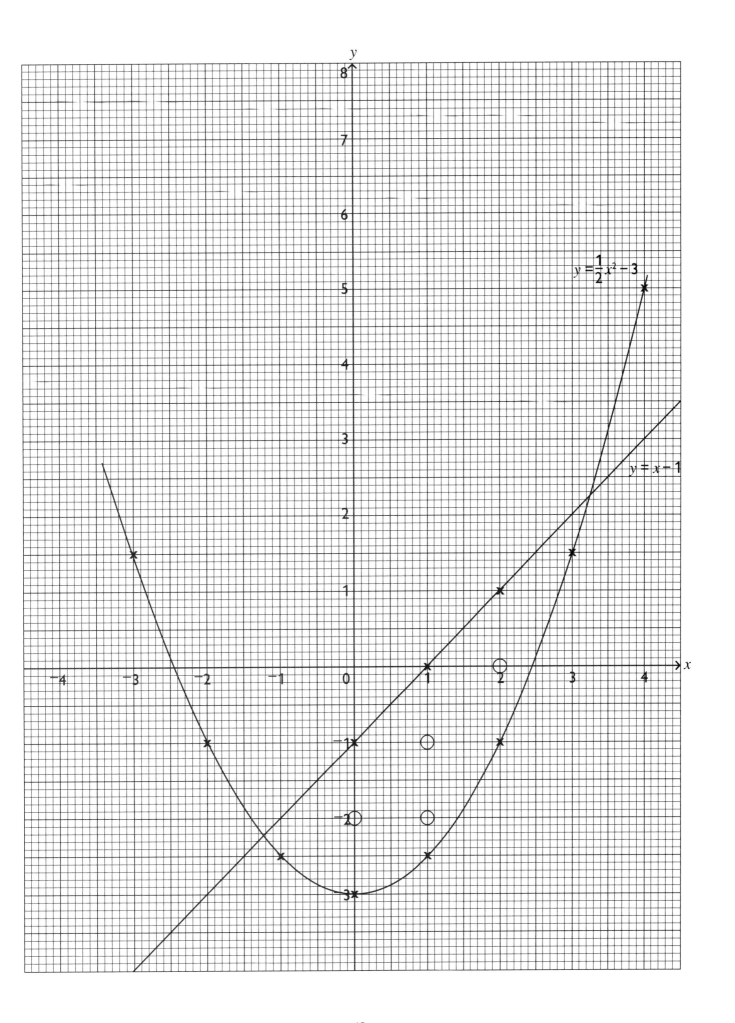

■■■ 18. (i)

x	−2	−1	$-\frac{1}{2}$	0	$\frac{1}{2}$	1	$1\frac{1}{2}$	2	3	4	(3)
y	8	3	$1\frac{1}{4}$	0	$-\frac{3}{4}$	−1	$-\frac{3}{4}$	0	3	8	

(ii) graph of $y = x^2 - 2x$ drawn (2)

(iii)

x	−3	0	3	(2)
y	0	3	6	

(iv) graph of $y = x + 3$ drawn (see over page) (1)

(v) (3.75, 6.75) (2)

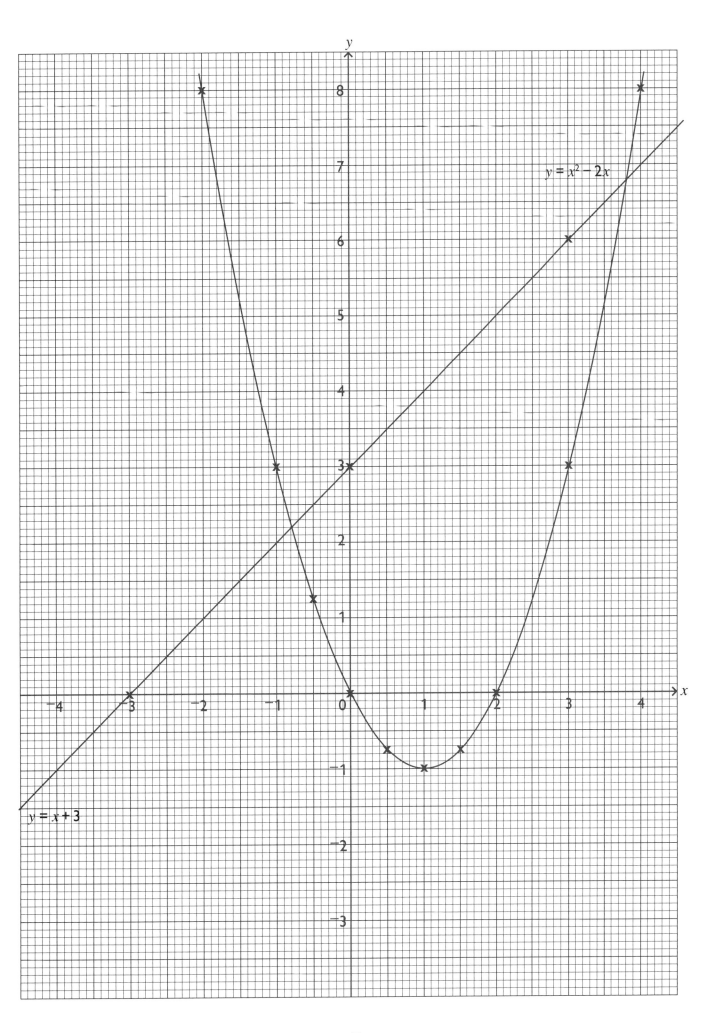

$y = x^2 - 2x$

$y = x + 3$

■■■ 19. (i) (a)

x	−2	−1	0	1	2
y	**4**	1	**0**	**1**	**4**

(2)

(b)

x	−2	−1	0	1	2
y	**−1**	**2**	3	**2**	**−1**

(2)

(ii) two graphs drawn (see over page) (4)

(iii) (−1.2, 1.5) (1.2, 1.5) (4)

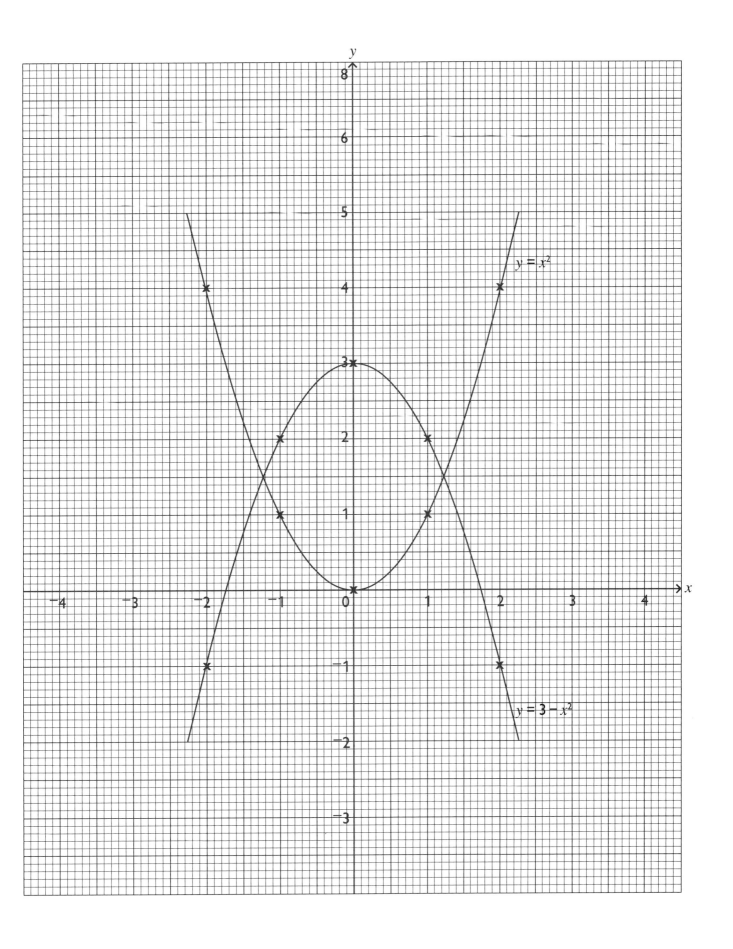

47

■■■ 20. (i)

(3)

input (x)	output (y)
‾1	0
2	6
4	10

(ii) graph of function drawn and labelled

(3)

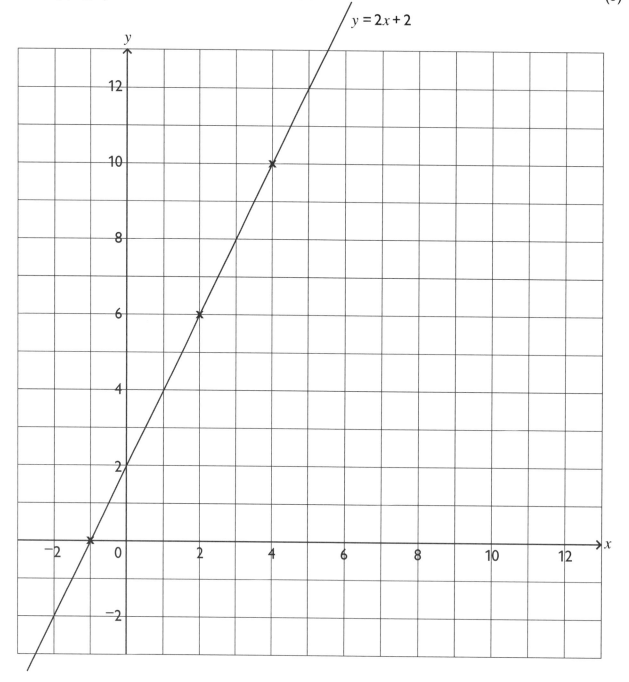

■■■ 21. (i) labels written on machine (2)

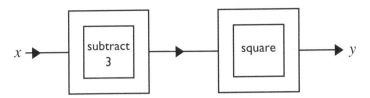

(ii) 13 (2)

■■■ 22. (i) (4)

x	⁻3	⁻2	⁻1	0	1	2	3
x^2	9	4	1	0	1	4	9
y	6	2	0	0	2	6	12

(ii) (a) y has its lowest value when x is $-\frac{1}{2}$ (1)

(b) the lowest value of y is $-\frac{1}{4}$ (1)

(iii) graph drawn (3)

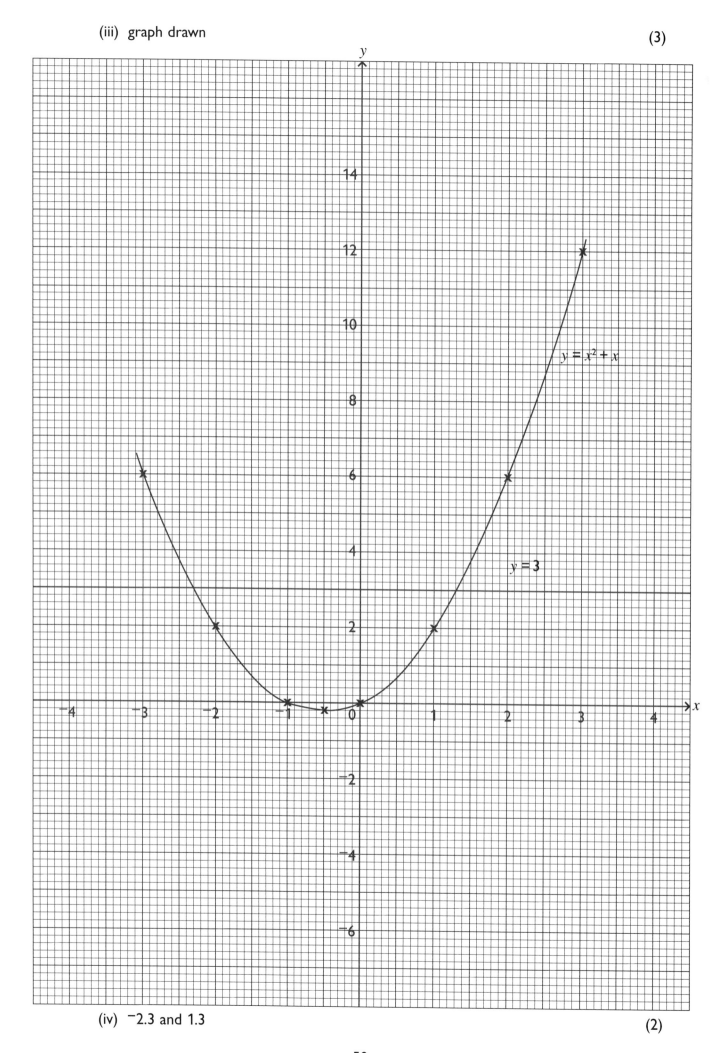

(iv) ⁻2.3 and 1.3 (2)

■ ■ ■ 23. (i) $x = \frac{1}{2}$ (1)

(ii) $(\frac{1}{2}, -2\frac{1}{4})$ (2)

(iii) (a) point plotted   (1)

     (b) graph drawn   (2)

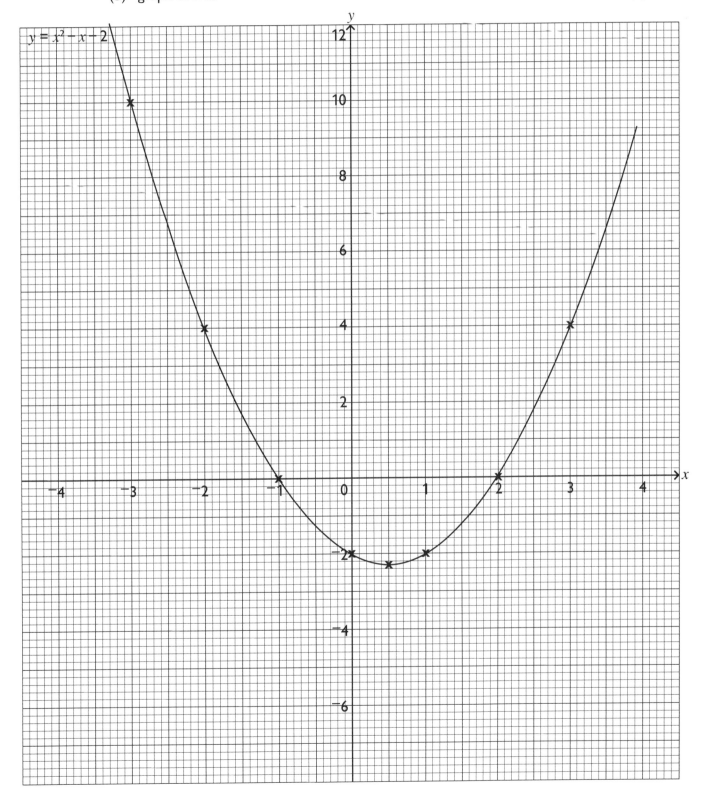

$y = x^2 - x - 2$

■■■ 24. (i) (5)

x	$^-3$	$^-2$	$^-1$	0	$\frac{1}{2}$	1	2	3	4
x^2	9	4	1	0	$\frac{1}{4}$	1	4	9	16
$\frac{1}{2}x^2$	$4\frac{1}{2}$	2	$\frac{1}{2}$	0	$\frac{1}{8}$	$\frac{1}{2}$	2	$4\frac{1}{2}$	8
$\frac{1}{2}x$	$-1\frac{1}{2}$	$^-1$	$-\frac{1}{2}$	0	$\frac{1}{4}$	$\frac{1}{2}$	1	$1\frac{1}{2}$	2
y	6	3	1	0	$-\frac{1}{8}$	0	1	3	6

(ii) graph drawn (3)

(iii) (a) (2)

x	$^-1$	0	2
y	3	2	0

(b) $y = 2 - x$ drawn (see over page) (1)

(iv) $(^-2.5, 4.4)$ $(1.5, 0.4)$ (2)

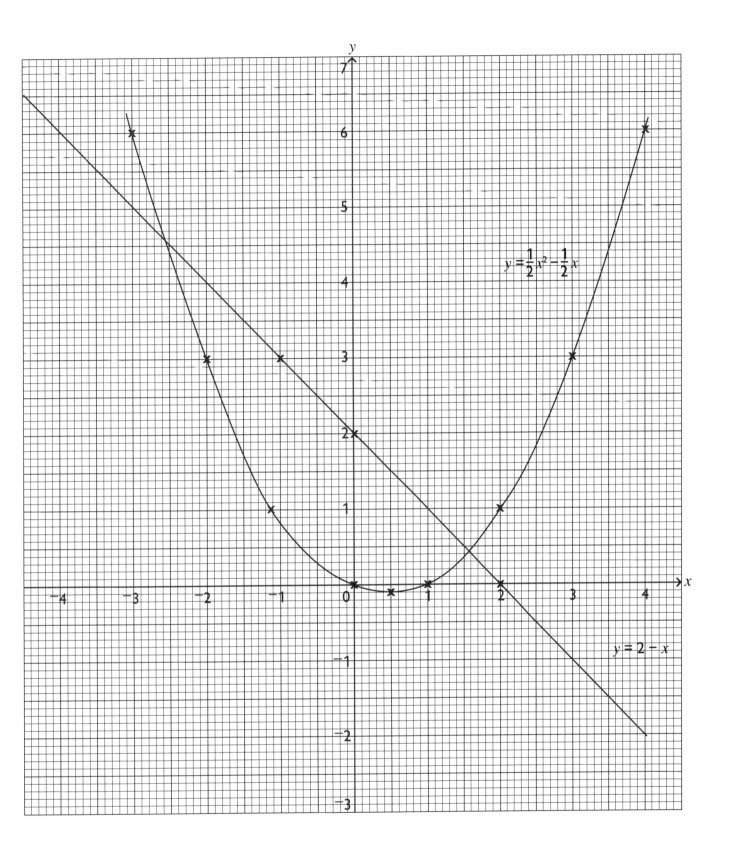

$$y = \frac{1}{2}x^2 - \frac{1}{2}x$$

$$y = 2 - x$$

■■■ 25. (i) tables completed

(a) Machine P: $y = x^2 - 1$ (2)

input (x)	output (y)
2	3
−3	8

(b) Machine Q: $y = (x - 1)^2$ (2)

input (x)	output (y)
2	1
−3	16

(c) Machine R: $y = x^2 - 2x + 1$ (3)

input (x)	output (y)
2	1
−3	16

(ii) $(x - 1)^2$ is equivalent to $x^2 - 2x + 1$ (2)

■■■ 26. (i) (a) $m + n$ (1)

(b) $n - m$ (1)

(ii) $m + n = 25$ (2)

(iii) $n = 16$ (3)

■■■ 27. $x = 12, y = 4$ (4)

■■■ 28. $a = 7, b = 2$ (4)

■■■ 29. (i) $2(x + y) = 22$ or $2x + 2y = 22$ and $x - y = 1$ (3)

(ii) $x = 6, y = 5$ (3)

■■■ 30. $x = 2, y = {}^-3$ (5)

■■■ 31. (i) $x + y = 43$ and $x - y = 30$ (4)

(ii) $x = 36.5, y = 6.5$ (3)

(iii) 237.25 (2)

32. (i) (a) 41 (2)

      (b) 54 (2)

  (ii) the 11th term 149 (3)

  (iii) the first term 9 (2)

33. (i) (a) $100x + 50y = 850$ (2)

      (b) $50x + 100y = 950$ (2)

  (ii) (a) $x = 5$ (2)

      (b) $y = 7$ (2)

34. (a) $x = \frac{1}{4}$ $y = 2$ (5)

  (b) (i) 17 (3)

     (ii) 731 (2)

Shape, space and measures

S1 Measures

1. (a) 350 cm   (1)

    (b) 73.6 cm   (1)

    (c) 4050 ml   (1)

    (d) 0.69 kg   (1)

2. 12.4 degrees   (2)

3. (i) 400 g   (2)

    (ii) 70 cm   (2)

    (iii) 8000 cm³   (2)

4. (i)   (4)

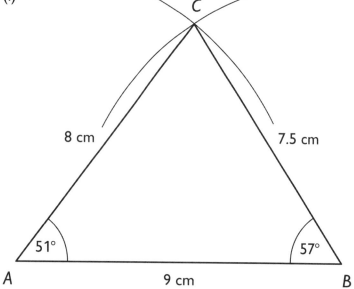

    (ii) (a) 57°   (1)

         (b) 51°   (1)

5.   (i)   (3)

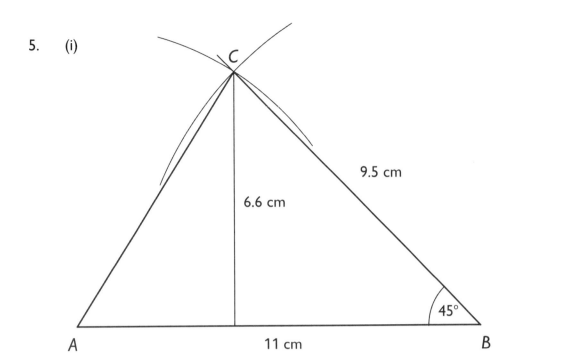

C

9.5 cm

6.6 cm

45°

A   11 cm   B

(ii)   6.6 cm   (1)

6.   (i)   30°, 60°, 90°   (2)

(ii)   (2)

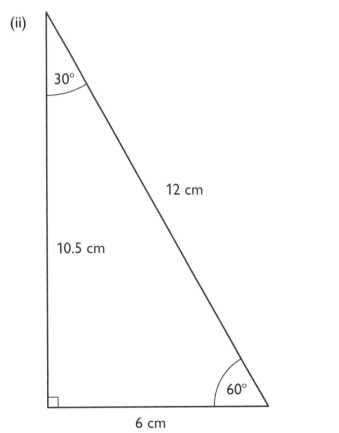

30°

12 cm

10.5 cm

60°

6 cm

(iii) 31.5 cm²   (2)

57

7.   (i)   (2)

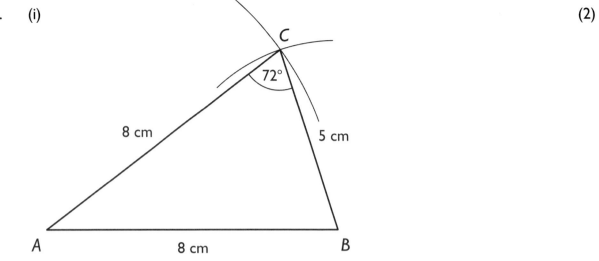

(ii) 72°   (1)

8.   (i)   (3)

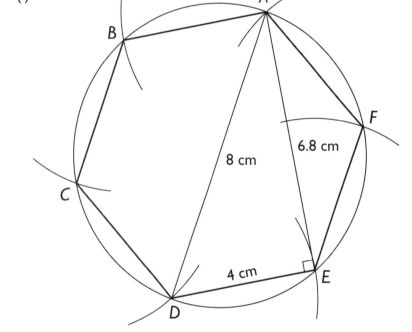

(ii)   8 cm   (1)

(iii) about 40 – 41 cm²   (3)

9. (i)   line *PQ*, 12 cm long, drawn   (2)

    (ii) point *R* marked, such that *PR* is 8 cm and *RQ* is 4 cm   (2)

    (iii) area represented   (3)

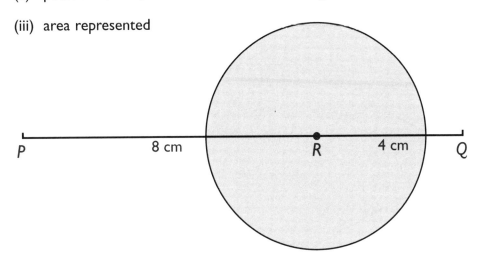

P   8 cm   R   4 cm   Q

10. (i)   (3)

    (ii) 5.7 cm   (1)

    (iii) (a) 22.8 cm   (2)

         (b) 32.5 cm²   (2)

11. (a) (i)   12 cm²   (2)

        (ii) 18 cm   (2)

    (b) (i)   14 cm²   (2)

        (ii) 22 cm   (1)

12. (i)   (3)

    (ii) 90 cm³   (2)

    (iii) 126 cm²   (4)

13. (i) 36 cm³   (2)

    (ii) 70 cm²   (4)

14. (i) 477 cm³   (3)

    (ii) (a) 250 cm³   (2)

          (b) 227 cm³   (1)

15. (i) 500 m   (2)

    (ii) 38 cm   (2)

    (iii) 3.25 km   (2)

    (iv) (a) 50 000 m²   (3)

          (b) 5 ha   (1)

◀■□	16.	(i)	36 mm		(2)
		(ii)	100 mm^2		(3)
		(iii)	150 mm^3		(2)
◀■□	17.	(i)	(a)	88 cm	(2)
			(b)	616 cm^2	(3)
		(ii)	(a)	462 cm^2	(2)
			(b)	300 g	(3)
◀■□	18.	(a)	1.54 m^2		(2)
		(b)	390 cm^3		(2)
■□	19.	(i)	14 m		(1)
		(ii)	280 m^2		(1)
		(iii)	154 m^2		(2)
		(iv)	56 m^2		(2)
		(v)	68 m^2		(3)
		(vi)	124 m^2		(1)
◀■□	20.	(i)	(a)	3.5 cm	(2)
			(b)	38.5 cm^2	(2)
		(ii)	423.5 cm^3		(2)
		(iii)	2.75 cm		(3)
◀■□	21.	(i)	(a)	18 cm^2	(2)
			(b)	30 cm^2	(2)
		(ii)	4.8 cm		(1)
		(iii)	(a)	30.1 cm	(3)
			(b)	10.0 cm	(2)
		(iv)	300 sheep		(2)
◀■□	22.	(i)	8 m/s		(2)
		(ii)	28.8 km/h		(3)
◀■■	23.	(a)	a solid shape which has:		
			● three or more parallel edges of equal length		
			● constant cross-section		(3)
		(b)	15.7 m^3		(4)

S2 Shape

1. (i) (2)

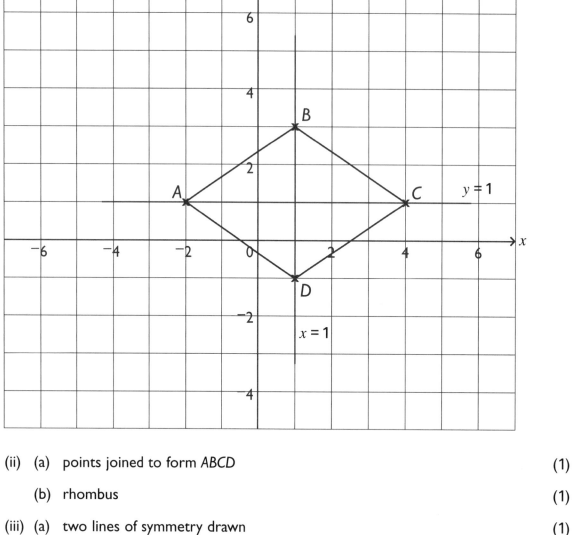

(ii) (a) points joined to form *ABCD* (1)

(b) rhombus (1)

(iii) (a) two lines of symmetry drawn (1)

(b) $x = 1$ and $y = 1$ (1)

(iv) order 2 (1)

(v) 12 cm² (2)

2. (a) (i) (1)

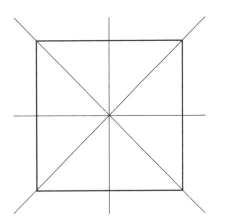

     (ii) 4 lines of symmetry drawn (2)

     (iii) order 4 (1)

  (b) (i) isosceles trapezium or kite sketched (2)

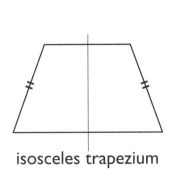

isosceles trapezium

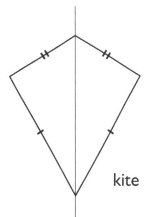

kite

     (ii) isosceles trapezium or kite (1)

3. (a) (i) (4)

5 cm

70°

5 cm

     (ii) rhombus (1)

  (b) (i) no lines of symmetry

       rotational symmetry order 2 (2)

     (ii) opposite sides parallel (1)

     (iii) opposite angles equal (1)

■■□ 4. (i) 45° (2)

(ii) 8 sides (2)

(iii) 1080° (1)

(iv) regular octagon (1)

■■□ 5. (a) 144° (3)

(b) (i) regular pentagon (2)

(ii) order 5 (1)

■■□ 6. (i) (a) 9 sides (1)

(b) 140° (1)

(c) 1260° (1)

(ii) (a) 40° (2)

(b) 30° (2)

7. (i) (a) 8 vertices (2)

(b) 12 edges (2)

(ii) (a) 10 cm^2 (2)

(b) 51.2 cm^2 (2)

(c) 20 cm^3 (2)

8. answers vary; examples: (2 marks each)

64

S3 Space

1.	(i)	50°		(2)
	(ii)	40°		(2)
	(iii)	140°		(1)
2.	(a)	(i)	48°	(1)
		(ii)	132°	(2)
	(b)	(i)	36°	(2)
		(ii)	108°	(2)
3.	(i)	125°		(1)
	(ii)	70°		(2)
	(iii)	70°		(2)
	(iv)	70°		(1)
	(v)	140°		(2)
4.	(i)	60°		(1)
	(ii)	120°		(1)
	(iii)	30°		(2)
	(iv)	90°		(2)
5.	(i)	(a)	35°	(1)
		(b)	25°	(1)
		(c)	110°	(2)
		(d)	120°	(2)
	(ii)	trapezium		(1)
6.	(i)	45°		(1)
	(ii)	145°		(2)
	(iii)	35°		(2)
	(iv)	235°		(2)
7.	(i)	35°		(1)
	(ii)	70°		(1)
	(iii)	110°		(2)

(iv) 80° (2)

(v) 145° (2)

8. (i) (a) 1 cm to represent 2 km (1)

(b) 1 : 200 000 (2)

(ii) diagram copied (2)

(iii) Rulerford marked (2)

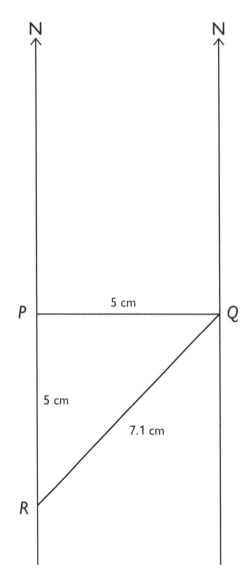

(iv) (a) 10 km (1)

(b) 14.2 km (2)

9. (i) *C* marked and north line drawn through it (1)

(ii) *L* marked (2)

(iii) *F* marked (2)

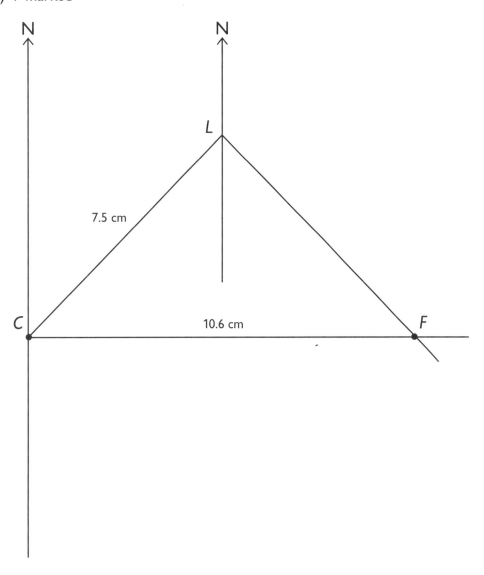

(iv) 106 m (2)

10. (i) (4)

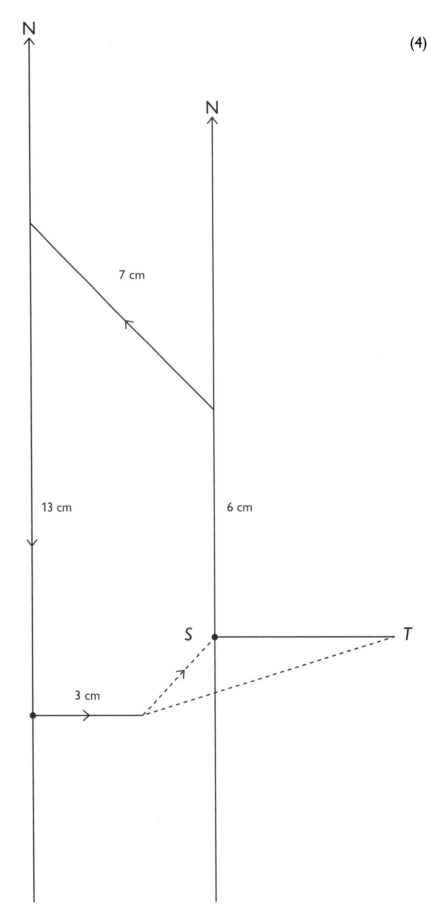

(ii) (a) 7 paces (2)

(b) approximately NE (2)

◀■□	11.	(i)	030°		(1)
		(ii)	108°		(2)
		(iii)	210°		(2)
◀■□	12.	(i)	100°		(2)
		(ii)	245°		(3)
◀■□	13.	(i)	route of boat drawn		(2)
		(ii)	position of W marked		(2)

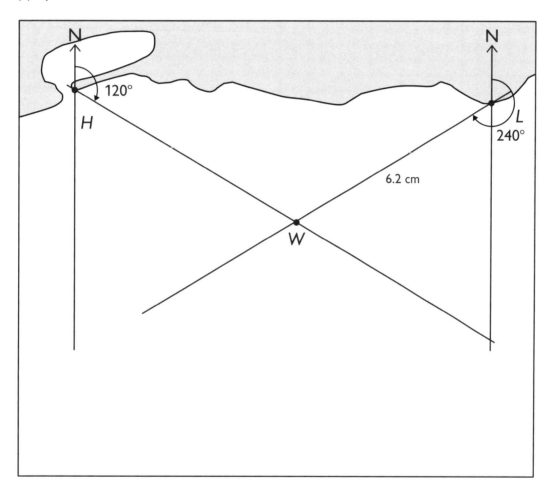

(iii) 310 m (3)

■■□ 14. (i) (4)

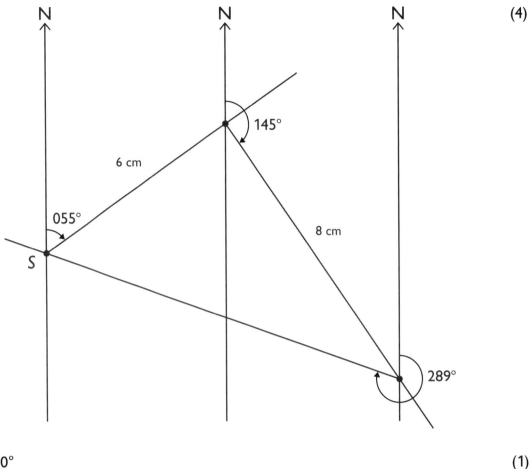

(ii) 90° (1)

(iii) 100 m (3)

(iv) 289° (2)

15. (i) triangle **A** drawn (2)

(ii) line $y = 2$ drawn (1)

(iii) triangle **B** drawn (3)

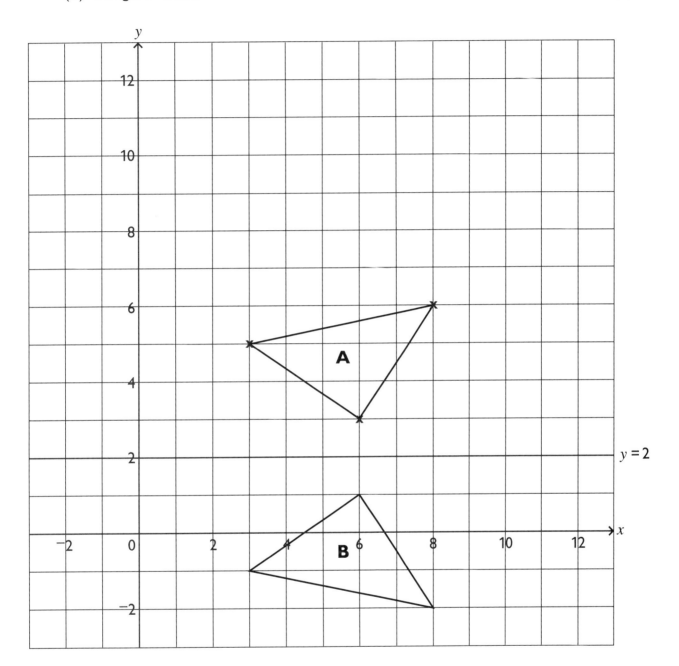

(iv) (3, ⁻1), (6, 1), (8, ⁻2) (3)

16. (i)   point A plotted   (1)

    (ii) point B plotted   (1)

    (iii) point C plotted   (1)

    (iv) (a) triangle ABC drawn   (1)

        (b) line $y = x$ drawn   (1)

    (v)   triangle $A^I B^I C^I$ drawn   (4)

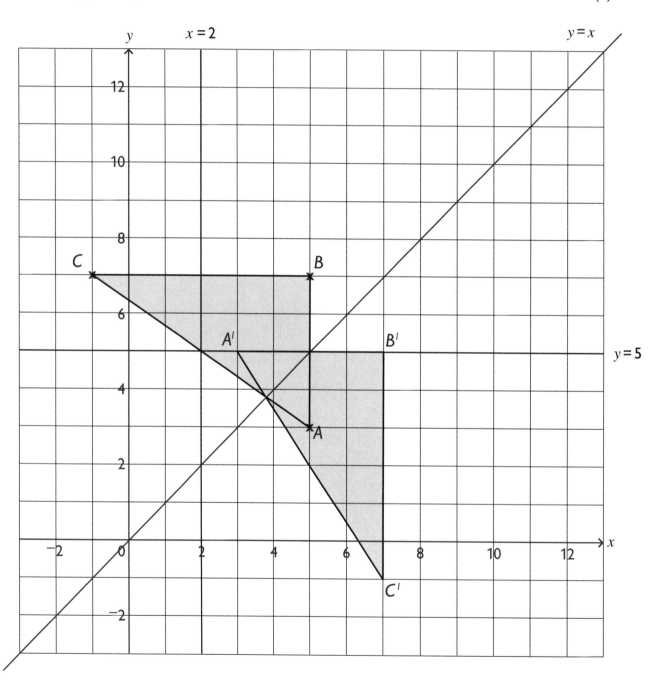

72

17. (i) points plotted and triangle **A** drawn (1)

(ii) line $y = 6$ drawn (1)

(iii) triangle **B** drawn (2)

(iv) triangle **C** drawn (2)

(v) triangle **D** drawn (1)

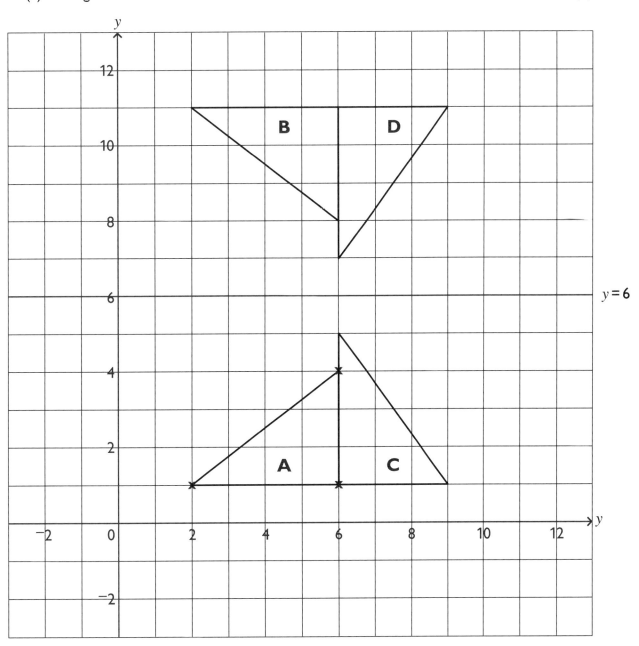

18. (i) triangle **P** drawn (2)

   (ii) triangle **Q** drawn (2)

   (iii) triangle **R** drawn (2)

   (iv) line $y = x$ drawn (2)

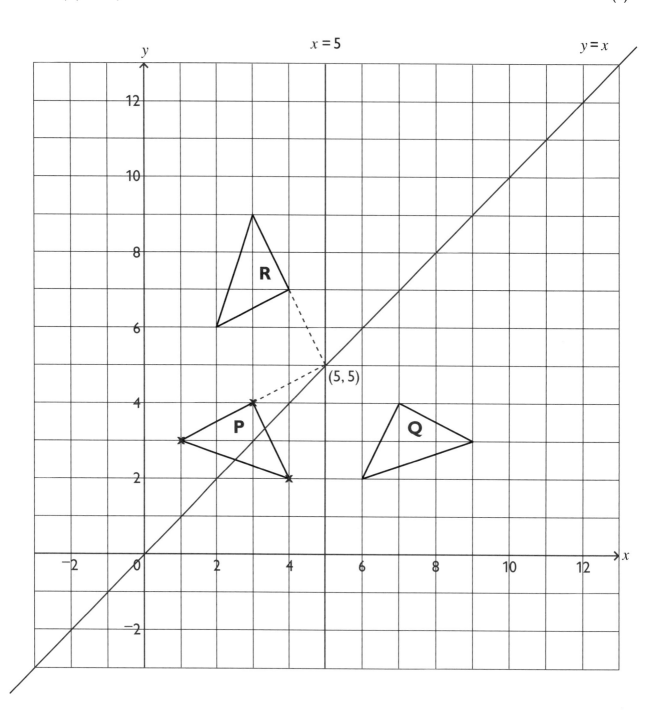

74

◀■□ 19. (4)

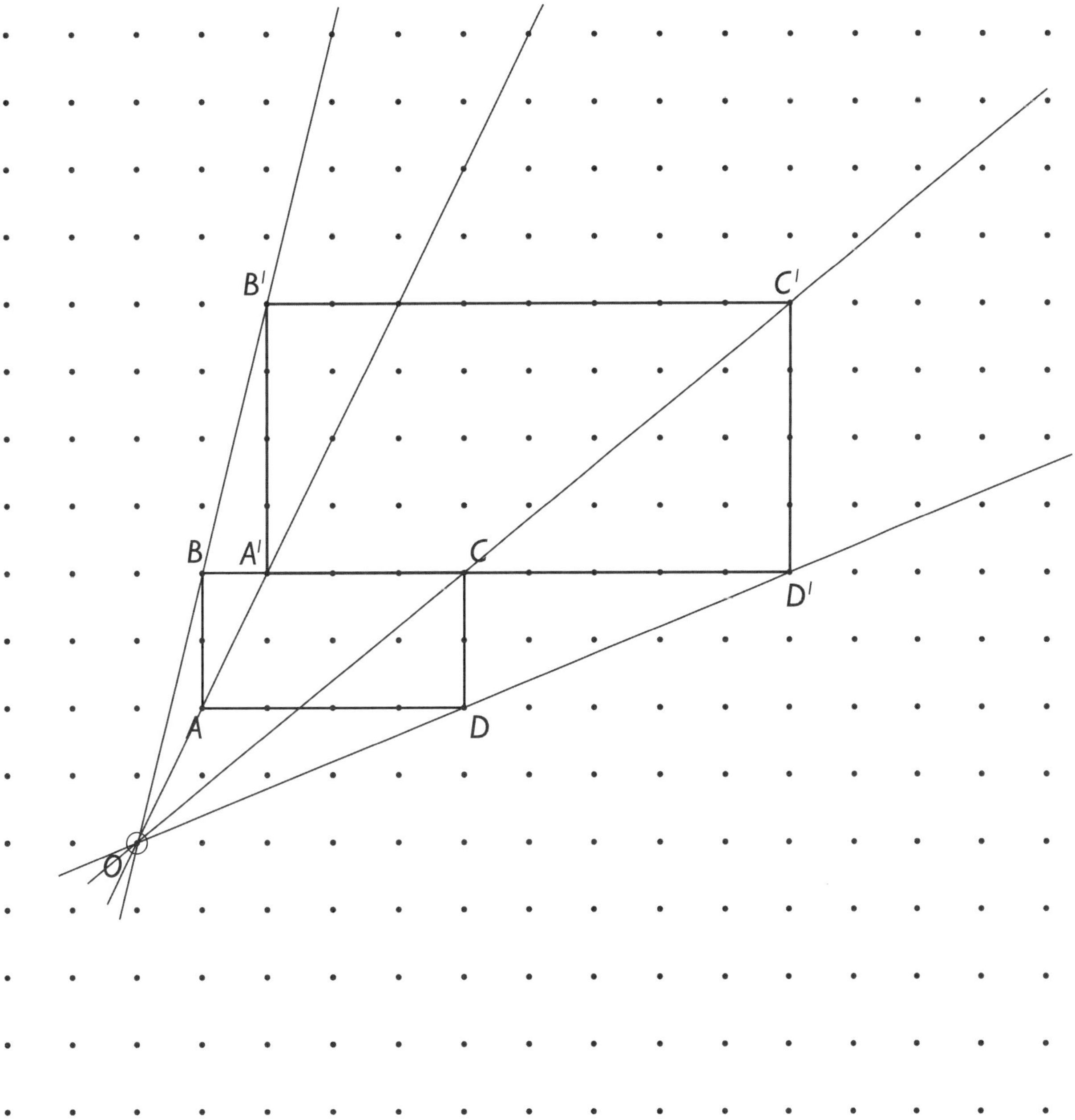

(i) (3)

(ii) 40 cm² (2)

(i)   (3)

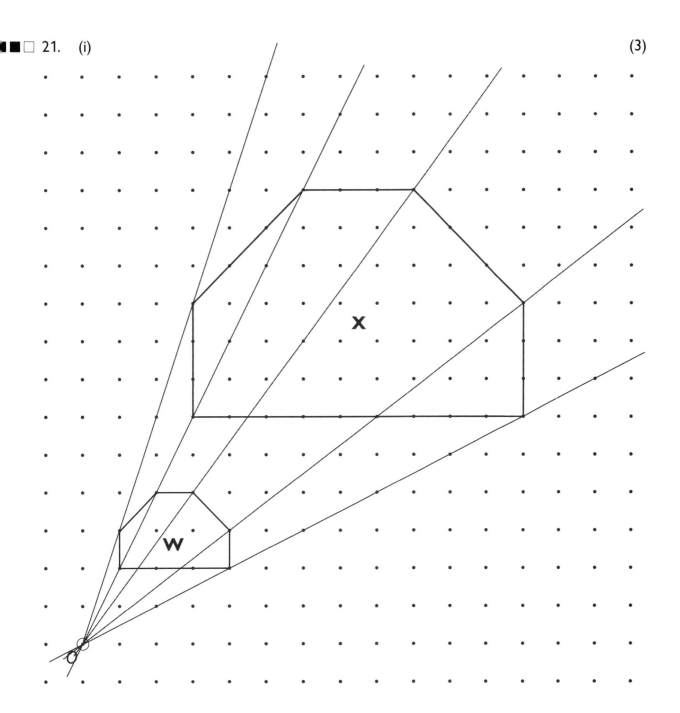

(ii)   5 cm² (2)

(iii) 45 cm² (2)

■■□ 22. (i) (3)

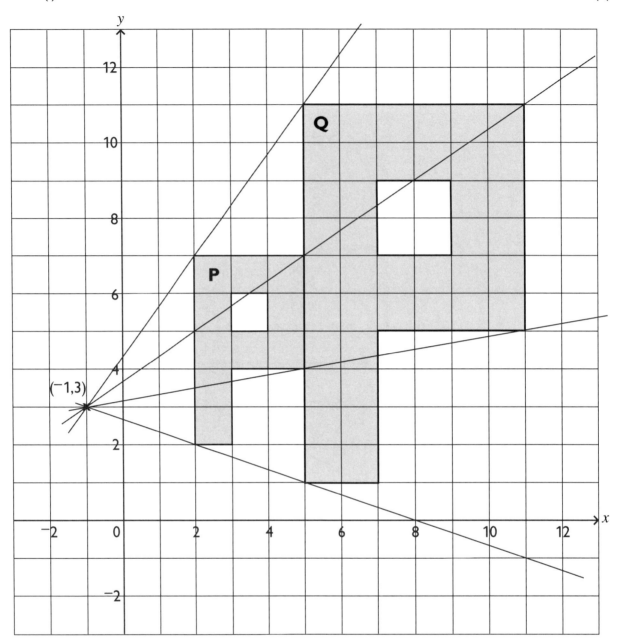

(ii) (a) 10 cm² (2)

(b) 40 cm² (2)

(i)   9 cm² (2)

(ii)   144 cm² (2)

(iii) (3)

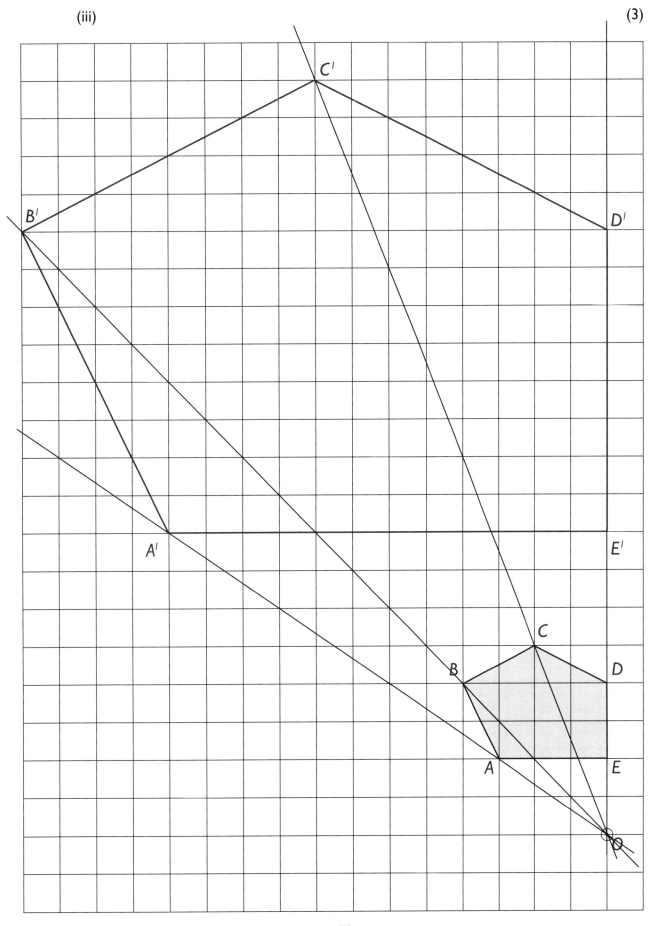

　(i)　(3)

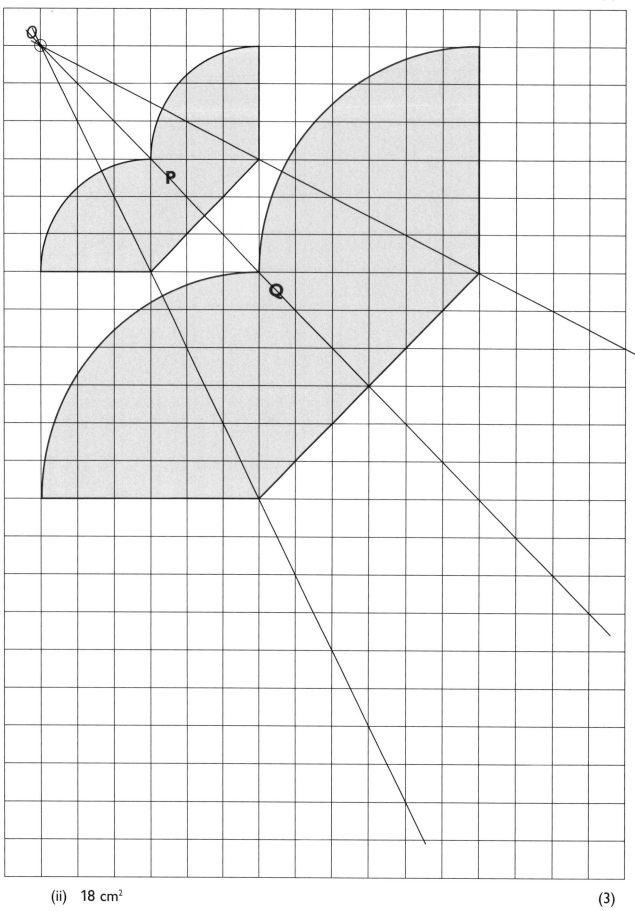

(ii)　18 cm^2　(3)

(iii)　72 cm^2　(2)

25. (i) (a) points plotted and *ABCD* drawn (3)

(b) *E* plotted and *DEA* drawn (1)

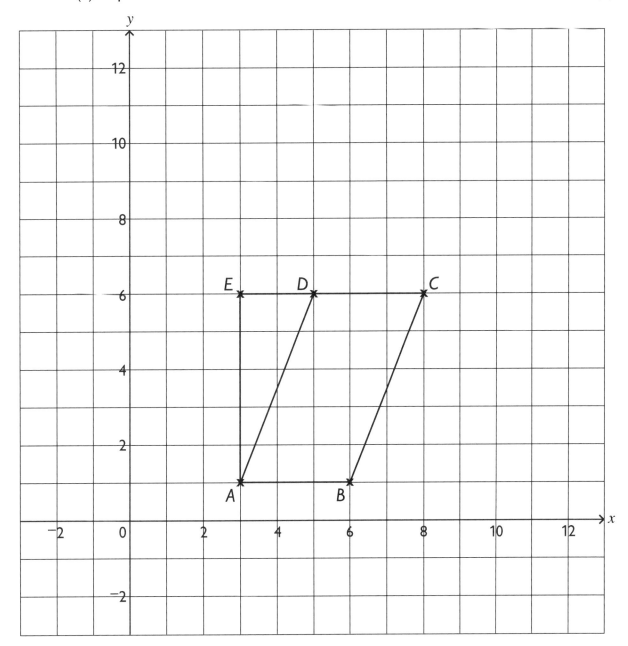

(ii) (a) 5 cm² (1)

(b) 15 cm² (1)

(iii) (a) 5.4 cm (2)

(b) 7.1 cm (2)

26. (i) 8.7 cm (2)

(ii) 9.6 cm (4)

■■■ 27. (i) 6 cm (2)

    (ii) (a) 7.42 cm (2)

        (b) 11.42 cm (1)

    (iii) 34.3 cm^2 (2)

    (iv) (a) 22° (3)

        (b) 44° (1)

        (c) 121° (2)

Handling data

D1 Data handling

1. (i) 16 (1)

   (ii) (3)

Number of chips	Tally	Frequency
10–12	IIII	4
13–15	卌 I	6
16–18	卌 IIII	9
19–21	卌	5
	Total	24

   (iii) (a) $\frac{7}{12}$ (2)

       (b) $\frac{1}{6}$ (2)

2. (i) (3)

Marks	Tally	Frequency
4	I	1
5	II	2
6	卌	5
7	IIII	4
8	II	2
9	II	2
10	II	2
	Total	18

(ii) range 6 (2)

(iii) (a) mode 6 (1)

(b) median 7 (2)

(c) mean 7 (2)

3. (i) (3)

Marks	Tally	Frequency
1	IIII	4
2	IIII IIII	9
3	IIII I	6
4	IIII IIII I	11
5	IIII IIII	10
	Total	40

(ii) (3)

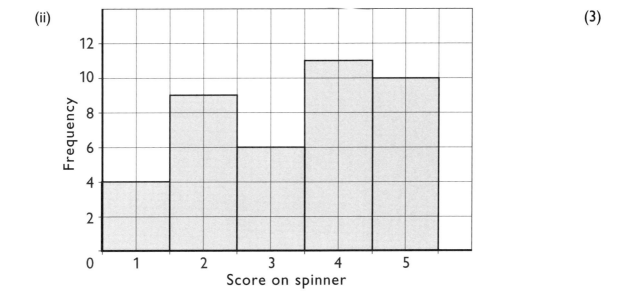

(iii) modal score 4 (1)

(iv) median score 4 (2)

(v) mean score 3.35 (3)

(vi) (a) $\frac{1}{2}$ (1)

(b) $\frac{3}{8}$ (1)

4. (i) 20 (2)

(ii) 50 (2)

(iii) 1 (1)

(iv) 2 (2)

(v) 2.5 (2)

5. (i) (a) 3 (1)

(b) 1 (1)

(c) 1.5 (2)

(ii) (a) Giants (2)

(b) Huskies (2)

6. (i) 8 (2)

(ii) 6 (1)

■■□ 7. (i) (a) 4.4 seconds (2)

(b) 35.15 seconds (2)

(c) 35.16 seconds (2)

(ii) (a) 6.1 m/s (2)

(b) 22.0 km/hour (2)

8. (i) 7 degrees (1)

(ii) 0 °C (1)

(iii) 0 °C (2)

(iv) ⁻0.6 °C (2)

9. (i) 4 parsnips (1)

(ii) (5)

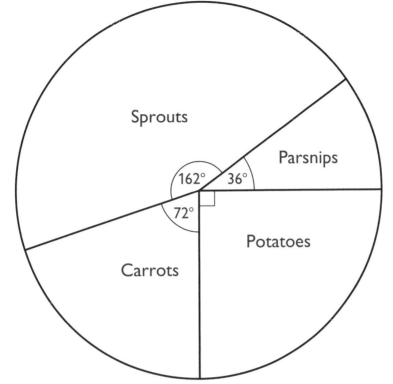

(iii) $\frac{3}{5}$ (3)

10. (i) 120° (1)

(ii) 10° (1)

(iii) (3)

Colour of coat	Number of people	Size of angle on pie chart
Blue	12	120°
Red	4	40°
Green	5	50°
Black	8	80°
Yellow	7	70°
Total	36	360°

(iv) 4 (2)

(v) (4)

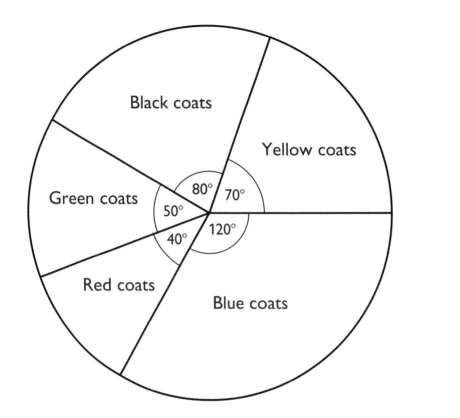

11. (i) 15° (2)

(ii) 135° (2)

(iii) $\frac{1}{4}$ (2)

12. (i) 20 (1)

(ii) (5)

Pop group	Number of children	Size of angle on pie chart
Scream	2	36°
Grubby	3	54°
Sloppydress	9	162°
Gruntalot	6	108°
Total	20	360°

(iii) (a) $\frac{3}{20}$ (2)

(b) $\frac{11}{20}$ (2)

13. (i) $1\frac{1}{2}°$ (1)

(ii)

Crop	Size of angle on pie chart
Oil seed rape	225°
Barley	90°
Wheat	45°

(3)

(iii) pie chart drawn and labelled fully   (3)

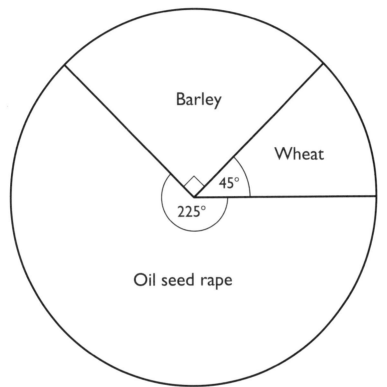

14. (i) (a) 48°   (2)

(b) 96°   (1)

(ii) (a) 36 children   (1)

(b) 216°   (2)

(iii) 6° represent each child   (2)

(iv)

Flavour	Number of children	Size of angle on pie chart
Vanilla	8	48°
Strawberry	16	96°
Mint	9	54°
Chocolate	27	162°
Total	60	360°

(2)

■■□ 15. (i) pie chart drawn with the data recorded below   (5)

Bulb type	Number	Size of angle on pie chart
Daffodil	48	120°
Tulip	18	45°
Crocuses	24	60°
Snowdrop	54	135°

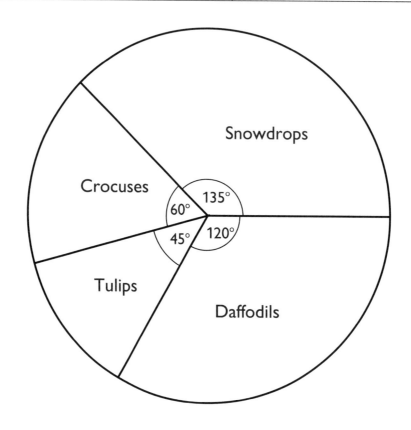

(ii) (a) 37.5%   (2)

   (b) 30 snowdrops   (2)

16. (i) (a) approximately $69 (2)

(b) £52 (2)

(ii) on flight better value (equivalent to £36) (2)

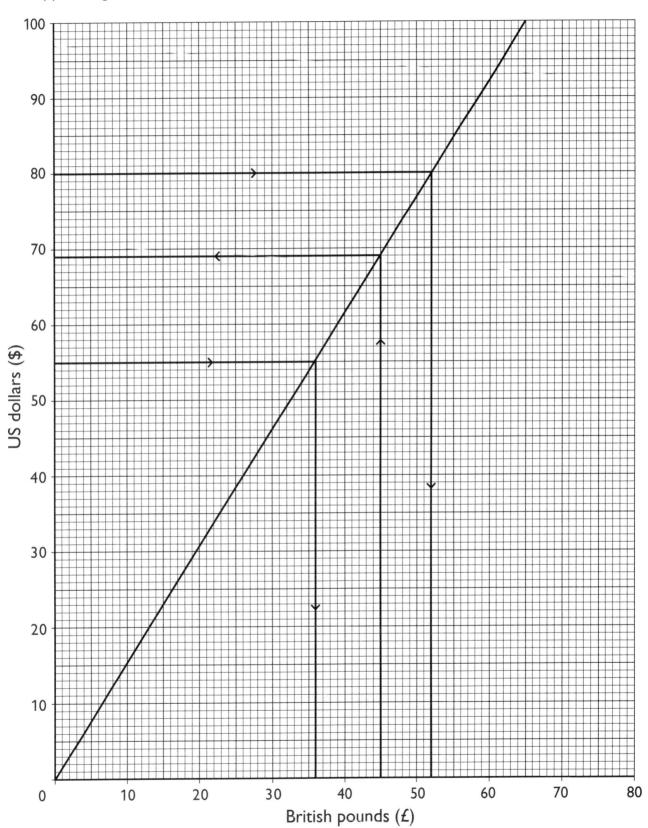

17.   (i)   (2)

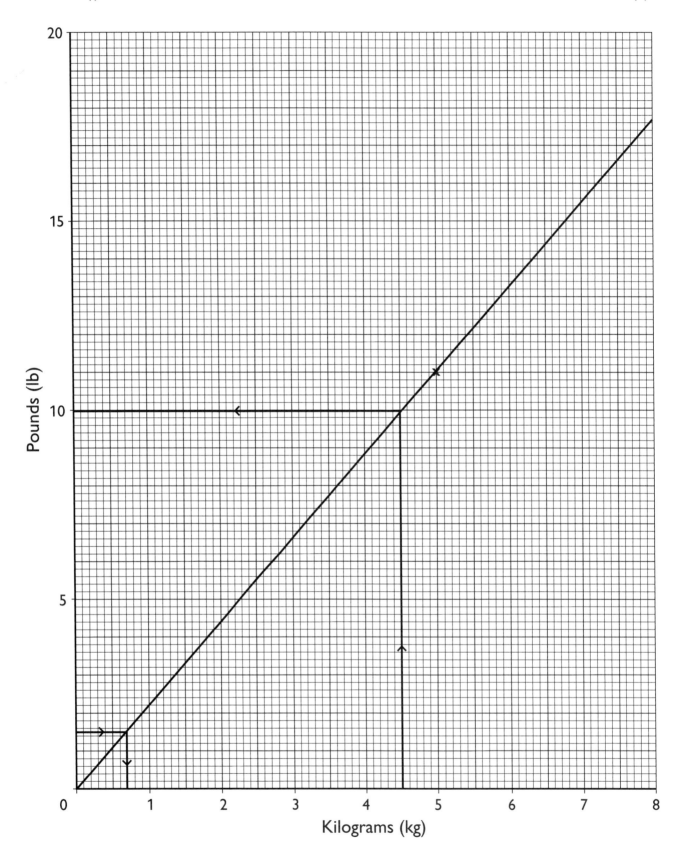

       (ii)   (a)   40 lb   (2)

              (b)   700 grams   (2)

18. (i) 260 euros (1)

(ii) (4)

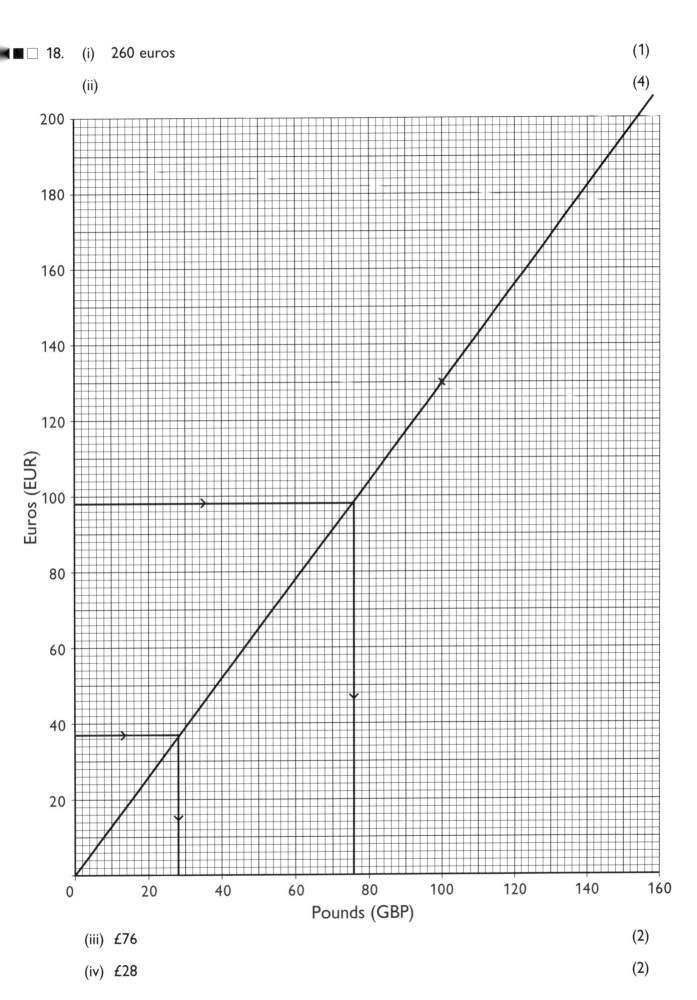

Euros (EUR) vs Pounds (GBP)

(iii) £76 (2)

(iv) £28 (2)

19. (i) 198 acres (2)

(ii) (3)

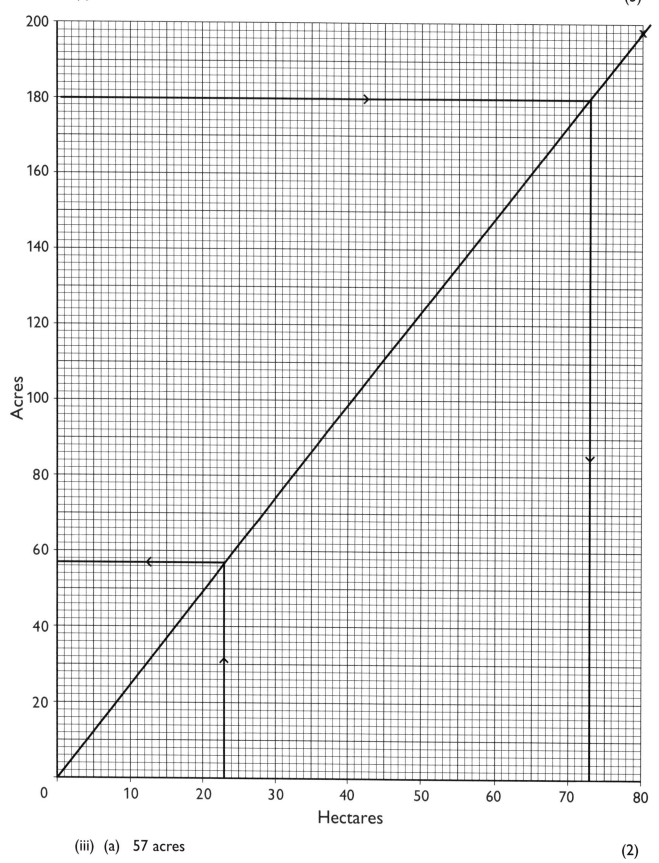

(iii) (a) 57 acres (2)

(b) 73 ha (2)

20. (i) £32 (1)

(ii) (2)

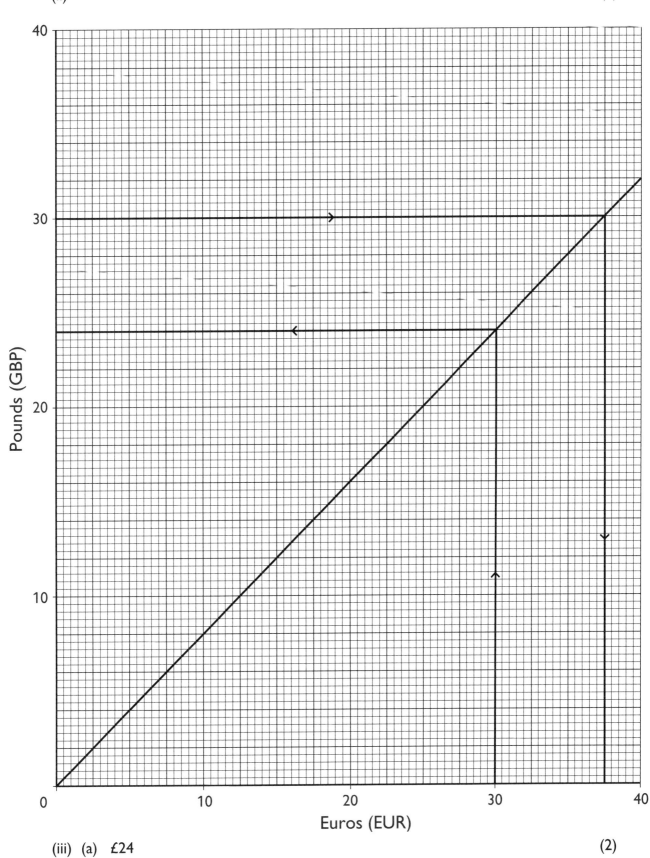

Pounds (GBP)

Euros (EUR)

(iii) (a) £24 (2)

(b) 37.5 euros (2)

21. (i) (5)

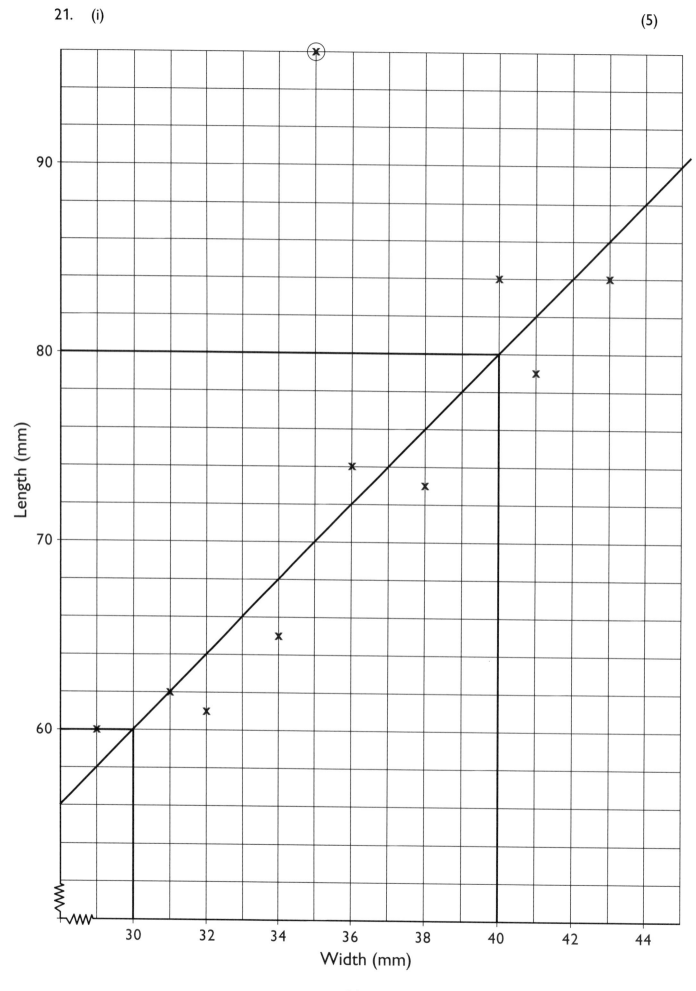

Width (mm)

(ii)   point circled   (1)

(iii) line of best fit drawn   (1)

(iv)   positive, fairly high, correlation   (1)

(v)   2 : 1

       readings taken vary; examples (30,60), (40,80)   (2)

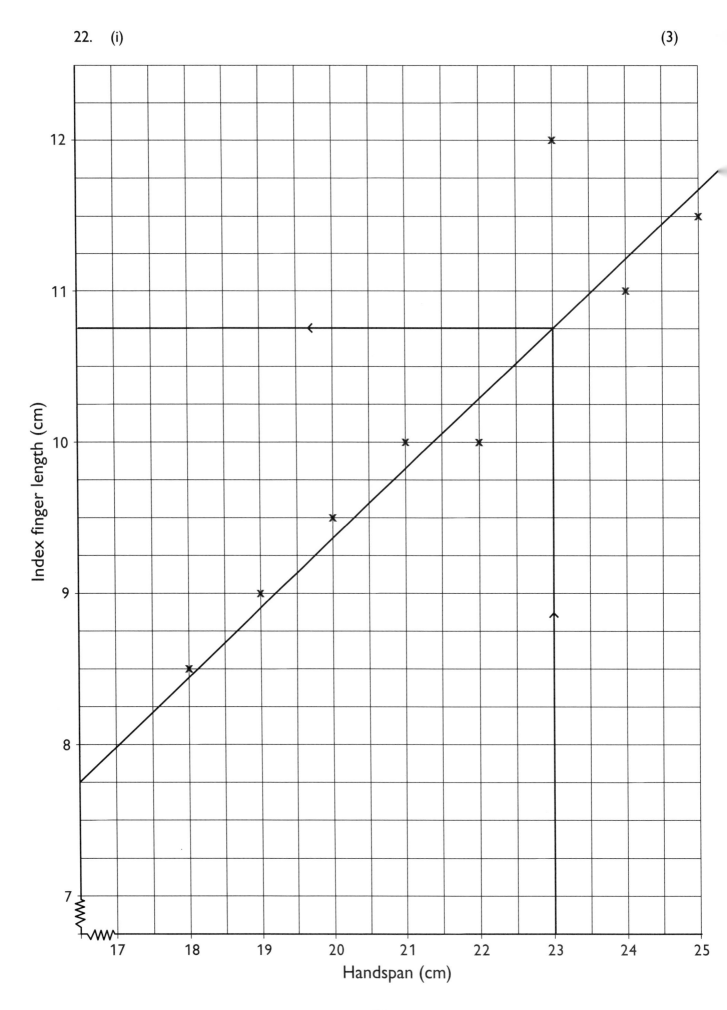

(ii) line of best fit drawn (1)

(iii) about 10.5–11 cm (2)

23. (i) (2)

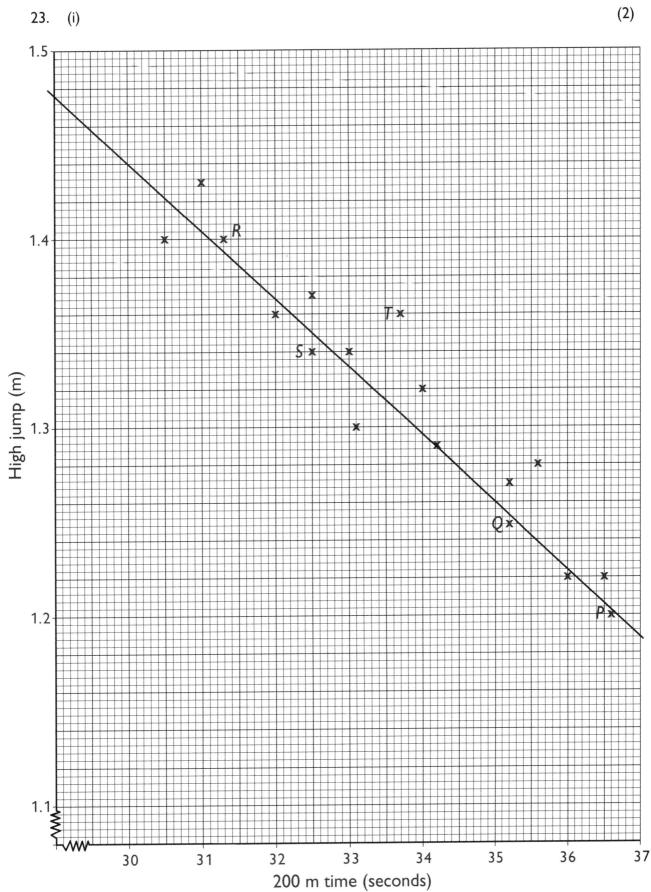

(ii) negative, high, correlation (1)

(iii) a good athlete will record a faster (lower) time and a higher jump (1)

(iv) line of best fit drawn (1)

(v) about 30.0 seconds (2)

(vi) about 1.28 m (2)

D2 Probability

1. (i)

H	and	1
H	and	2
H	and	3
H	and	4
H	and	5

T	and	1
T	and	2
T	and	3
T	and	4
T	and	5

(2)

(ii) (a) $\frac{3}{10}$ (1)

(b) $\frac{1}{5}$ (1)

2. (a) (i) (3)

	H	E	N	R	Y
B	BH	BE	BN	BR	BY
R	RH	RE	RN	RR	RY
I	IH	IE	IN	IR	IY
A	AH	AE	AN	AR	AY
N	NH	NE	NN	NR	NY

(ii) $\frac{2}{25}$ (2)

(iii) $\frac{12}{25}$ (2)

(b) 16 (2)

3. (i)   (3)

	score on pentagonal spinner				
score on square spinner	×	**1**	**2**	**3**	**4**	**5**
	1	1	2	3	4	5
	2	2	4	6	8	10
	3	3	6	9	12	15
	4	4	8	12	16	20

(ii) (a) $\frac{1}{10}$ (2)

(b) $\frac{3}{10}$ (2)

(c) $\frac{3}{10}$ (1)

(d) $\frac{3}{10}$ (2)

(iii) $\frac{7}{20}$ (2)

4. (i) $\frac{1}{5}$ (2)

(ii) $\frac{19}{25}$ (2)

5. (i) (a) $\frac{1}{49}$ (1)

(b) $\frac{24}{49}$ (2)

(c) $\frac{15}{49}$ (3)

(ii) (a) $\frac{1}{48}$ (1)

(b) $\frac{1}{2}$ (2)

6. (i) (a) $\frac{1}{6}$ (1)

(b) $\frac{1}{3}$ (2)

(c) $\frac{1}{2}$ (2)

(ii) (a) 20 times   (1)

(b) 40 times   (2)

(iii) 420   (2)

7. (i) (a) $\frac{1}{3}$ (2)

    (b) $\frac{2}{3}$ (2)

    (ii) (a) $\frac{1}{2}$ (1)

    (iii) $\frac{5}{11}$ (2)

8. (i) (a) $w + g$ (1)

    (b) $w - g$ (2)

    (ii) (a) $\frac{w}{w + g}$ (1)

    (b) $\frac{g}{w + g}$ (1)

    (iii) $\frac{g - 1}{w + g - 1}$ (2)

9. (i) (a) $\frac{1}{10}$ (1)

    (b) $\frac{1}{5}$ (1)

    (c) 0 (1)

    (ii) (a) $\frac{1}{9}$ (1)

    (b) $\frac{1}{9}$ (1)

    (c) $\frac{2}{9}$ (2)

    (iii) (a) $\frac{2}{5}$ (2)

    (b) $\frac{1}{10}$ (1)

    (c) $\frac{1}{5}$ (2)

    (d) $\frac{3}{10}$ (1)

10. (i) (a)

	boy	girl
do not like 'hide and seek'	1	2
like 'hide and seek'	3	6

answers may look different

(b)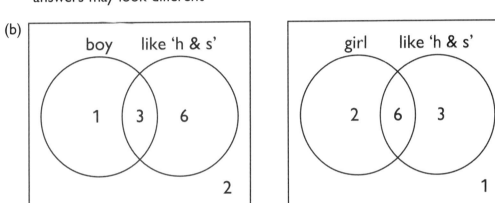

answers may look different

(ii) (a) $\frac{1}{4}$

(b) $\frac{1}{6}$

11. (i) (a) A J N O

(b) A E I J M N S

(c) B C D F G H K L P Q R T U V W X Y Z

(2)

(2)

(2)

(2)

(1)

(1)

(2)

101

(ii)

(4)

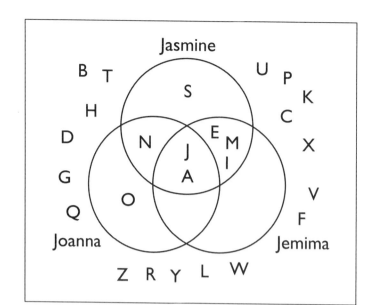

(iii) (a) $\frac{9}{13}$

(2)

(b) $\frac{3}{13}$

(2)